For Ann,
now you in
know all about
me. Curtis

My First 85 Years

An Autobiography

By Curtis C. Harlin, Jr.

Copyright © 2008 by Curtis C. Harlin, Jr.

ISBN 0-7414-5014-3

Published by:

INFINITY
PUBLISHING.COM

1094 New DeHaven Street, Suite 100
West Conshohocken, PA 19428-2713
Info@buybooksontheweb.com
www.buybooksontheweb.com
Toll-free (877) BUY BOOK
Local Phone (610) 941-9999
Fax (610) 941-9959

Printed in the United States of America

Printed on Recycled Paper

Published November 2008

Dedicated to the memory of my father,
whose love for the family first interested
me in knowing about my family and its history

Preface

Why would an ordinary man write an autobiography? It is understandable that a famous person would write about himself or herself. Most of us are interested in the details of our Presidents' lives, famous actors and actresses, or other distinguished persons. But an ordinary man—who is interested in what he did or said?

I believe that the ordinary man or woman has more to tell about himself or herself than is commonly thought. In fact, I suspect that the ordinary person's experiences are of interest to the masses because, with few exceptions, members of the masses are ordinary people too and can relate to those experiences.

So why am I writing about myself? It is not that I think my experiences are exceptional or that my accomplishments are so great. No, it is not out of egotism, nor trying to create an image of myself that is not true. A major reason is that I think I have a story to tell that in many ways is typical of my generation. Having lived through the Great Depression and World War II, I am of what Tom Brokaw calls "the greatest generation." Those of my generation who read this may say, "Yes, I did that," "I remember that," "That also happened to me." In recalling those experiences they may feel pride or remorse, love or hate, joy or sadness, but above any emotion, they will know that they are a part of the past and in some way contributed to whatever it means to them. I hope that those of you who are not of my generation, who read my story, will see something of the past, from the perspective of an ordinary person that you may not have seen before.

More personally, I hope that my relatives and friends may have some interest in what kind of a person I was, good or bad. I would appreciate having an account of my father and mother and their antecedents. I hope my children's children might have the same interest.

I want this account to be as factual as possible. It may not always be as complete as I would like it to be, because much of the story is from memory. Where records were available they were used, but otherwise most of the story is from my memory. I may not remember every detail of my past experiences, but the things I have written about really did happen.

I take full responsibility for what is written. I have not intentionally shown anyone in a bad light but have tried to recount everything honestly and fairly. Neither have I tried to portray myself better or worse than I am. I have tried to include all significant events regardless of whether they were good or bad.

This is my story. Those of you who read it, many or few, I hope receive some enjoyment, some understanding, a better feeling for yourself, and, above all, some laughs. After all, life is too serious to be taken too seriously.

Acknowledgment

Many people, through the years, have encouraged me in this writing. The first of these was in a writing class that I attended in 1991 in Arlington, Virginia. The instructor's encouragement and advice led me to seriously undertake this project. I have attended other writing classes since then and each one further encouraged me to continue with this writing. The helpful suggestions of the instructors, as well as fellow students, although unnamed, are gratefully acknowledged.

Portions of the book have been read by various friends and family members. Among these are: Hazel Foltyn, Charles Schmidt, Sandy Kiessling, Don Butkovic, and my wife Mary. These, and others that I may have forgotten, made valuable contributions which I gratefully acknowledge.

My thanks go to Carrie Worthington who edited the final manuscript. Her meticulous work revealed errors of grammar and punctuation, and her suggested changes are greatly appreciated. Her work made the final product more readable and enjoyable.

Much of the historical information contained in Chapter I and the genealogy information up to and including the birth of my great grandfather John Curtis in 1816 was taken from or is based on information from *History and Genealogy of the Harlan Family* by Alpheus H. Harlan. Without this valuable reference the early history of the family would be incomplete. Family information, following the birth of John Curtis Harlin, was compiled from old letters, public documents, and other information from family members and friends. My niece, Hazel Foltyn, added much information from her work in updating the family record.

The encouragement and comments and contributions of information and corrections of all those who are named, and any that I have inadvertently overlooked, are acknowledged, with much gratitude, without which this effort would not have succeeded.

Contents

I

Before My Time

What does an ordinary man have to show for his "three score and ten"? Will those who follow him be aware that he passed this way? Outside of his immediate family, and possibly a few close friends, he is soon forgotten. His grandchildren may or may not have a clear memory of him, depending on how close they were during his lifetime. Beyond their generation he is likely to be only a faceless name from the past.

It seems the further removed we are from our ancestors, the more curious we are about them. There is something in our makeup that causes us to want to know who we came from and what our antecedents were like. To satisfy this innate curiosity, I go back to seventeenth century England.

The Harlins began as the Harlands of England, a Yorkshire family. Records speak of the Harland estates of Sutton, Huby, and New Parke north of York. Sutton Hall, some eight miles north of York, was in the family before the Restoration.[1] Huby, and possibly New Parke, were granted to a certain Captain Richard Harland about the close of the civil wars.[2] Some thirty or forty miles north of York is a vast moor, a part of which, centuries ago, was called "Harland's Moor." On the east and west sides of this moor there were about thirteen thousand acres, all of which belonged to a James Harland.

---

[1] In 1660 the monarchy of Great Britain was restored with the return of Charles II to the throne.
[2] The wars between the Parliamentarians and the Royalists, 1642-1648.

1

My earliest ancestor, of which there is record, is James Harland, Yeoman and member of the Episcopal Church, who was born about 1625 in "Bishoprick, nigh Durham, England." Tradition says that his father's name was William. There is no record of James' wife, but it is known that he had at least three sons: Thomas, George and Michael.

My lineage proceeds from the son George, who was born about 1650 "...Nigh Durham, in Bishoprick, England." He was baptized at the Monastery of Monkwearmouth in "Oald England ye 11th Day First Month 1650."[3] Monkwearmouth Monastery was founded by Benedict Biscop in the year A.D. 672. It is situated in a town by the same name in the east division of Chester, County Durham. In 1790 the building was destroyed by fire, destroying the records of the family prior to that time.

In 1988, I had the great pleasure of visiting Monkwearmouth. My father had a copy of the *History and Genealogy of the Harlan Family*, by Alpheus H. Harlan. In this book there is a picture of, and information about, the old church that was a part of the monastery. To most Harlans/Harlins a visit to the old monastery is like a religious pilgrimage. My wife Mary and I landed in London, rented a car, and took a leisurely drive north: our destination, Monkwearmouth. We found the old church without too much difficulty and had a nice visit with the Vicar, The Reverend Martin Turner, and took a tour of the church. Above ground only the porch and west wall of the original Saxon church remain. It is said that the porch is one of the finest 7th-century porches in Britain. The church was restored through the years and is now an active parish of the Church of England known as Saint Peter's Church.

As a young man, George, a Yeoman like his father, with his brothers and others, moved to Ireland and settled in County

---

[3] The common names of months and days of the week were considered pagan by the Quakers, who used such terms as "First day" and "Second month." Also, prior to 1751, March was the first month of the year.

Down. Sometime before 1678 George apparently converted to Quakerism.

In the 1650s, George Fox founded The Religious Society of Friends, or Quakers, in England, in protest against the domination of the established church by the state and because of the leanings of the church toward Roman Catholicism. In the years that followed, the Quakers were severely persecuted by both the Church of England and the Puritans. During this time, many Quakers fled to Ireland because of the persecution. Everything points to the immigration of George and his brothers taking place during that time.

While living in Ireland, George was married to Elizabeth Duck, by ceremony of Friends, in the Ninth Month, seventeenth day, 1678. During the time George and Elizabeth lived in Ireland, they had four children. During their marriage they had a total of nine.

In 1687 George and Elizabeth, their four children, and George's unmarried brother Michael, immigrated to America and settled in William Penn's Colony. William Penn had joined the Quakers in 1666 and in 1681 obtained the charter from King Charles II for Pennsylvania. Pennsylvania was established in 1682, as a "holy experiment," on religious principles. In the following years this new land attracted thousands of immigrants from Europe who sought greater religious and political freedom as well as a chance for more prosperous lives. The English Quakers were by far the most important of the early groups that settled along the Delaware River in the southeast part of the Colony. George and Michael were in this group.

George had bought land within the County of New Castle prior to coming to America. The family landed at the town of New Castle, which is now in the state of Delaware, and settled near the present town of Centerville. George lived there for several years, but about 1698 he moved his family higher up Brandywine Creek where he had purchased land.

They settled in what is now Pennsbury Township, Chester County, Pennsylvania, but at the time was known as Kennett Township.

George, soon after arriving in America, became one of the foremost citizens of the colony. In 1695 he was one of the provincial governors of the "three lower counties," now the state of Delaware, and was a member of the Colonial Assembly in 1712.

After coming to America, George and Michael dropped the "d" from Harland. Today the majority of the descendents spell the name "Harlan." George died in the Fifth Month 1714 and was buried in the new burying ground on Alphonsus Kirk's land beside his wife, Elizabeth, who preceded him in death. This burial ground was later called Center Meeting Burying Ground.

The first of my ancestors to be born in America was Samual Harlan. Samual, the grandson of George, was born about 1722 in Kennett Township, Chester County, Pennsylvania. His father Aaron was the fourth child of George and Elizabeth, born in Ireland two years before the family came to America. Samuel's mother, Sarah Heald, married Aaron in a ceremony of Friends at Newark Meeting, New Castle County, Delaware, in 1713.

Samuel was a Quaker before his marriage to Elizabeth Hollingsworth in 1745. Apparently Elizabeth was not a Quaker, as they were married in Holy Trinity Church, Wilmington, Delaware. This old stone church was built in 1698 and is believed to be the oldest Protestant church in North America still in use for worship. The church was originally built as a Swedish Lutheran Church, but is now Episcopalian.

The Society of Friends was a "peculiar people" with strict rules of order. Punishment by disownment was common for breaches of disciplines, such as marrying out of the society. Following his marriage, Samual was called before the congregation on charges of being married by a priest (Quakers have no clergy) and excessive drinking. In 1746 at Central Meeting, he was disowned from the society. Elizabeth apparently became a Quaker sometime after their wedding and remained in good standing throughout her life. There is no record of Samual ever returning to the church.

My father, Curtis, was a very proud and somewhat self-righteous man who thought the worst that could happen was to bring discredit to the family name. Many times I have heard him say that the only black mark in the family history was his ancestor who was kicked out of the church for marrying outside the church. He never mentioned that Samual was also an excessive drinker, because my father was very much against consumption of alcoholic beverage in any form. At every opportunity he would brag that never in his life had he had a drink of anything alcoholic.

In 1753, Samual and his brother Aaron, two years his junior, with some other members of the family, moved to Chatham County, North Carolina. Before that time, all of the family had remained in southeast Pennsylvania and Delaware, the area where they originally settled. Later, Samual moved on to the Union District of South Carolina where he lived as a farmer the rest of his life.

The next major move was made by another Samual Harlan, a grandson of the discredited Samuel. The younger Samuel was born in Union District, South Carolina, July 31, 1778. He married Nancy Fitzpatrick in 1800, and immediately moved to the southern part of Kentucky that is now Monroe County. Records show that Samual and his wife Nancy were Baptists. Before that time, most of the Harlans had been Quakers since coming to the New World. Samual and Nancy had 10 children, including John Curtis, my great grandfather, who was born in Monroe County Kentucky, July 14, 1816.

An interesting story about Nancy Fitzpatrick has been handed down in the family. In the early days of immigration to this country, the ships were made of wood and usually traveled in convoys. Many times the fragile ships, if caught in a storm, would break up with the loss of many lives and property. As the story goes, a convoy of ships was caught in a great storm off the east coast of America and all were wrecked. The only known survivor was a small baby girl who was washed to shore on some of the debris, her identity unknown. She was taken in by a farmer named Alexander Fitzpatrick, given his name, and raised as his own child in the Union District of South Carolina. That baby girl was Nancy Fitzpatrick.

The records show that the children of Samual and Nancy spelled their names three different ways: Harlan, Harlin, and Harling.[4] According to an account given by a niece of one of my grandfather's brothers, the different spellings were an outcome of the War Between the States.

At the time of the Civil War, many of the Harlans lived in Monroe and Macon counties, adjacent counties of Kentucky and Tennessee, respectively. With its divided loyalties, Kentucky chose to remain neutral during the war while Tennessee sided with the South. It seems that the Harlans were divided over secession: those who lived in Kentucky were for the North while those of Tennessee supported the South. It is known that at least one of the sons of John Curtis, Stephen, fought with the Confederacy and was seriously wounded in the battle of Iuka, Mississippi.

During the war, the Harlans of Kentucky did not experience hardships to the extent their relatives in Tennessee did. The Tennessee Harlans went through deprivations and hardships of all kinds, including loss of property. This caused much bitterness in the family, resulting in the name-change. My great grandfather, John Curtis, was one of those who spelled his name "Harlin."

---

[4] Alpheus H. Harlan, *History and Genealogy of the Harlan Family,* p. 226.

John Curtis married Mary Meador in Monroe County, Kentucky, about 1835. They had a total of nine children. Sometime during their marriage they moved to Tennessee, and the last three of their children were born in Macon County, Tennessee, including my grandfather, Varney Silas Harlin, who was born November 11, 1854.

When my grandfather was about 21 years old, he moved to Texas. I don't know the circumstances or if he was alone in this move. His father and mother apparently remained in the Tennessee-Kentucky area and are both buried in the Gamaliel, Kentucky, cemetery. Whether or not other members of his family accompanied him is not known. It is known that other Harlins and Harlans, probably cousins and aunts and uncles, were in Texas in those early days. Also, at least one of his brothers moved to Texas. His younger brother, Oliver Kansas, is listed as a member of the Bois d'Arc Baptist Church, located in Hill County, Texas, in 1880.

During this time, my grandfather lived in two different places in Texas, although the sequence is not clear. He probably settled in Fannin County first, because he married Sarah Elizabeth Stringer in Savoy, Texas, August 8, 1878. She was the only child of Ruben E. Stringer and Sophia Northworthy Stringer. After their marriage they moved to Hill County, Texas, where their first child, Oliver Ewing, was born in Hillsboro in 1879. Their second child, Zilla, was born in 1881, also in Hillsboro.

When my grandparents married, my grandmother was only sixteen years old. My grandfather was seven years older than she. In later years when anyone mentioned that she was only sixteen when she married, she would say, "...no, I was going on seventeen."

During the next few years, the family made several moves. The third child, John Silas, was born in Saltlick, Tennessee, in 1884, followed by William Joseph in Monroe County, Kentucky, in 1886, Nina in Macon County, Tennessee, in

1889 and my father, Curtis Chester in Monroe County, Kentucky, in 1892. The last child, Birdie, was born in Fannin County, Texas, in 1900.

My grandmother's father, we called him Grandpa Stringer, was born in Simpson County, Kentucky, October 20, 1837. He was the son of James and Mary Stringer of Alabama. Nothing is known of his parents beyond this. After the birth of their daughter (my grandmother) in Simpson County, February 20, 1862, the family moved to Texas and settled in Fannin County where Grandpa Stringer was a successful merchant and banker. His wife Sophia, my great grandmother, died in 1906 and was buried in the Commerce, Texas, cemetery.

My grandfather Harlin was a farmer most of his life. During the time he lived in Fannin County, Texas, however, he operated a general store in Savoy in partnership with my great grandfather Stringer. I have heard my father recall the time his father ran the store. He also had farming interests at that time.

Much is said today about how mobile our society is, but the family of my grandfather Harlin did its share of moving. Maybe they were the forerunners of today's mobile society. Between the times my grandfather and grandmother married in 1878 and 1902 when they moved to Oklahoma, they moved at least seven times and lived in three different states. During that time they lived in Texas, Tennessee, and Kentucky. Traveling those days was a far cry from our modern jet age. The primary modes of transportation were horse-drawn wagon and horseback. One wonders why the family made so many moves under such difficult conditions.

During those years, the family was growing and it seemed that each move included an additional family member. By the time of the last move back to Texas from Kentucky, a trip of several hundred miles, there were six children. My father, Curtis, under two years of age, was the youngest. A move of that many people, ranging in age from adulthood to infancy, by wagon and horseback, under the conditions of the time, was no small undertaking.

After returning to Texas, the family lived in Fannin County about eight years, before crossing the Red River into Indian Territory in 1902. This was five years before statehood in 1907, the year Oklahoma was created from Indian and Oklahoma Territories. The Kawah-Commanche area of the Indian Territory was opened up in 1902, and my grandfather bought land in the area which would become Cotton County, near Temple, Oklahoma.

The move was made by horse-drawn wagons and on horseback. My grandparents and the girls traveled by wagon. My Aunt Birdie was born after the family returned to Texas, and she was a baby at the time of this move. In addition to the usual furniture and supplies, the family had cattle to move. The boys traveled on horseback and drove the cattle. My father was only 10 years old at the time. I have heard my grandmother tell how she worried about my father, at such a young age, traveling all that distance on horseback with the older boys. The trip was made without mishap though, and the family settled down on their new farm located three miles north of Temple.

The first order of business was to build a house. All of the lumber for the house had to be brought by wagon from Addington, a distance of about 30 miles. The house had two stories with five rooms on the first level and two large rooms upstairs. I remember it well, having visited my grandparents many times in my youth. The upstairs was always filled with mystery, and I would approach it with fear and excitement when I was young.

One of the upstairs rooms was occupied by Uncle Kansas, Grandfather's younger brother. His wife died in 1907, at the age of 42, and having no children, he made his home with my grandparents the rest of his life. He was a great reader. I remember cautiously climbing the stairs to see him sitting in his cane-bottom chair, leaning against the wall reading his book, and enjoying his twist chewing tobacco. He would peer at me over the top of his wire-rimmed glasses, and though he would not say a word, I would scurry back down the stairs. He was a quiet man, spent much time alone, and would not even think of harming anyone. I realized later that he was just having his fun with us children.

The other large upstairs room was full of all kinds of fascinating objects. By the time I knew the place, it had long since been made the repository for all kinds of discarded items. I spent many an hour prowling through this marvelous, dusty collection of so many things I had never seen before. I guess today they would be prized antiques.

It was in this house that the family grew up and where my grandparents lived the rest of their lives. The two oldest children, Aunt Zillah and Uncle Ewing, didn't live in this home very long as they both married in January 1903. The others lived there from 3 to 24 years before marrying. Some even lived there after marriage.

In the early years of statehood, Oklahoma established a very good rural school system. A schoolhouse was located every three miles. My grandfather provided the location for one of them on the southwest corner of his farm. The school was named Pioneer School. All of the younger children attended this one-room school, and very often the school teacher would stay with my grandparents, as their house was the nearest to the school. The children would go to high school in Temple after finishing grade school at Pioneer.

This part of Oklahoma was fairly well populated in those days, much more so than today. The state was divided into sections of one-mile square and quarter sections of 160 acres. Practically all of the farms consisted of a quarter section of land with a family living on it. There was a minimum of four families living on most sections. The average school served nine sections, which could include about 36 families. Considering the size of families in those

10

days, this would be a goodly number of students in one room.

The schoolhouses not only provided a place for the children to learn their ABCs, they were also the center for most community activities. Social events were often held in the schoolhouse, as well as other community meetings. Very often church services were held in the buildings, in areas that did not have an established church. This was the case at Pioneer. I remember attending services when I would be visiting my grandparents. Of course, those days were before the separation-of-church-and-state issue was so heated. The people, in their ignorance, did not know that such public facilities should not be used for religious purposes.

Following Grandpa Stringer's retirement, he came to live with my grandparents, my grandmother being his only child. He was quite wealthy, and as each of his grandchildren married, he gave them a 160-acre farm for a wedding present.

My mother, Bertha May Dodd, and my father, Curtis, were married January 4, 1914. She was the daughter of Rufus Elmer Dodd and Mary Catherine Conner Dodd who, at the time of my parents' marriage, lived on their farm in the Valley View community about five miles east of Walters, Oklahoma. Their home was three miles north of the Harlin home.

My grandfather Dodd was born at Metropolis, Illinois, just across the Ohio River from Kentucky, June 22, 1866. When he was about six months old his mother died, and his father's sister Rebecca and her husband Robert C. Hill, took him to raise. They lived in Carroll County, Tennessee. He and my grandmother were married in Weatherford, Texas, January 20, 1889. My grandmother Dodd was born April 19, 1871, in Dongola, Illinois. Soon after their marriage, they moved to the Burneyville Community in Indian Territory, near present-day Ardmore, Oklahoma.

My mother was born in the Burneyville Community, September 28, 1895. She had an older sister Clennie and a younger brother Lloyd, who were also born in the Burneyville Community. My grandparents' first child, Jessie, was born in 1891 but died when he was only two years old. Mother's sister, Clennie, died as a young woman, before I was born, leaving two children.

Her brother Lloyd caused the family much grief. At one time he was in prison. I was probably in my early teens at the time. The family didn't discuss my Uncle Lloyd so I know very little about him. I know that my mother endured much sorrow because of her brother.

I don't know how long my grandmother and grandfather Dodd lived in the Burnesyville Community, but sometime after 1900 they moved to the farm located five miles east of Walters, in the Valley View community, where they lived when my mother and father were married.

Grandfather Dodd, even as a young man, did not have good health. He suffered from respiratory problems, probably asthma or emphysema. I remember his always having trouble breathing. On December 16, 1910, they sold their farm equipment and livestock at a public auction and moved to Alamagorda, New Mexico, because of my grandfather's health. I remember hearing my mother talk about their move to New Mexico. The family did not live in New Mexico very long. They had returned to Oklahoma, and were once again living on their farm east of Walters, when my mother and father married in 1914. They must not have sold the farm when they moved to New Mexico.

The Valley View community, where my mother lived, had a Baptist Church in addition to a schoolhouse. My Grandfather Dodd was a deacon in the church and the family worshiped there regularly. The Valley View Baptist Church was the closest church to the Harlins' home so they also attended there occasionally.

My father's claim to fame is that he was the inventor of an improved cow yoke. I am sure I hear a loud chorus of "What is a cow yoke?" from the reader. Most cow pastures, and some other enclosures for cattle, are surrounded by barbed wire fences. Usually, the fences are constructed with three to five horizontal wires stretched around the parameter of the pasture, fastened to posts set in the ground about 10 to 20 feet apart. Very often a cow will stick her head between the fence wires to graze outside her allotted area. I guess this is the origin of the old saying, "The grass looks greener on the other side." If the wires of the fence are spaced too far apart, are loose, or not attached securely to the posts, the wayward cow can make her way through the fence to freedom. Sometimes cows can become professionals at escaping from their pastures and become very difficult to keep at home. So here is where the cow yoke comes in: it is a device that fits around the cow's neck to prevent the critter from getting through a fence.

My father's cow yoke was fabricated from thin steel bars into a circular collar that fit loosely around the cow's neck. Extending a length of about 12 to 15 inches from the collar were two metal strips terminating with forked projections. These two metal strips were fastened on opposite sides of the collar so that one extended above the cow's neck and the other extended downward below the cow's neck. On the top and bottom of the collar were sharpened projections. The collar was hinged in the middle so that when a cow tried to put her head through a fence, the hinged collar would rotate and cause the sharp projections to stick the cow's neck and, being rather uncomfortable, would cause the cow to back away from the fence.

My father was granted patent number 1122389 for his revolutionary invention December 29, 1914. I don't know anything about the production of the yoke or how many were produced. I doubt that my father realized a significant amount of money from them. After all, even in 1914, a cow yoke was not an item that every household had to have.

Nevertheless, the effort probably meant a lot to my father at the time, and he did receive a very impressive looking certificate from the Commissioner of Patents, complete with gold seal.

When my mother and father married, Grandpa Stringer gave them their 160-acre farm for a wedding present, as was his practice. The farm was located in the Empire Community, which was eight or nine miles north of where my father was raised. That is where my parents lived during the first years of their marriage.

Not too long after moving into their new home on their new farm, an event occurred which probably changed the course of their lives forever—not only their lives but the lives of their children and their children's children. (It is interesting to speculate, although probably a useless exercise, on how things might have been had certain events in our lives not occurred.) This event was the drilling of the discovery well for the Empire oil field on my parents' farm.

In those days, in such virgin fields, the wells came in with a spectacular geyser of oil. They were referred to as gushers. This is the way the wells came in on my parents' farm. I have heard my father tell of the excitement of watching the wells come in and the good feeling of being sprayed by gushing black gold. I don't know exactly how many wells were drilled on my parents' farm but it was at least four. I have obtained well logs from the Oklahoma Corporation Commission for four wells that were drilled while my parents owned the property. Whatever the exact number, it was enough to make them well off, financially, in a short time.

In June 1993, I made a trip to Oklahoma, and after searching the records in the Cotton County courthouse, I found my way to the Empire Community and to my parents' farm. There was no house or other buildings remaining, but I did see three oil wells that were still in production. I didn't determine if these were some of the original wells or not. But it was interesting to know that after over 70 years there was still oil under the old farm.

On December 26, 1915, my sister, Hazel Lorene, was born on the farm in the Empire Community. Her timing was just a little bit off, having missed being a Christmas present by only one day. Hazel lamented that she never really had a birthday celebration because her birthday was so close to Christmas. I do know that my mother always saw that one gift was reserved for Hazel's birthday. Nevertheless, the excitement of Christmas probably always took away from a true birthday celebration.

My father always loved livestock and at an early age was engaged in buying and selling cattle. I have heard him speak of shipping cattle to the Kansas City market when he was still in his teens. His love for cattle pulled the family from their oil-soaked land in Oklahoma to the wide-open spaces of the Texas panhandle.

About 1918, the family moved to Plainview, Texas. My father traded the 160 acres in Oklahoma for a 1,650-acre ranch near Plainview. This land had been a part of the Goodnight Ranch, which was one of the large west Texas ranches of early days. The native buffalo grass was ideal for range cattle, and the soil was rich and fertile. In those days, probably the greatest resource was the abundant groundwater of the region. The source of the groundwater was the great Ogallala aquifer that extends from Nebraska to southern west Texas.

Before the development of extensive irrigated farming in the Panhandle region, water wells in the high plains were free-flowing artesian. Not only was the water abundant, it was very economical since it required minimum pumping. My father's operation included both cattle and irrigated farming. Although he managed the day-to-day operation of the ranch, we always lived in Plainview.

In the early 1920s, and possibly before, two of my father's brothers, Silas and Joe, and their families, also lived in the Plainview area. I am not certain who came first, but I suspect that the brothers followed my father after he acquired the ranch.

While living in Plainview, Uncle Joe's wife died during the flu epidemic of 1923. She was my Aunt Laura, whom I don't remember. Their youngest child, Anna Laura, was only two months old when her mother died. Uncle Joe was left with eight children ranging in age from two months to 15 years.

Uncle Joe was a remarkable man. He never remarried and always kept his children together. They were all successful and married well, several of them being college graduates at a time when a college education was not as common as it is today. I know that two were graduate engineers and at least two were teachers. Uncle Joe could not have done what he did without help. After Aunt Laura's death, her mother, Martha Jane Brown, went to live with the family. The children called her Grandma Brown. She helped Uncle Joe rear his children; she, also, must have been a remarkable person.

Up to my generation, the Harlins were largely agricultural people. There were a few exceptions, but the majority of the people were engaged in farming or ranching. My father's oldest brother, my Uncle Ewing, moved to Commanche, Oklahoma, after his marriage to Nora Frank James, and he owned and operated the first Coca Cola bottling works in the southwest part of Oklahoma. But in a few years he moved to the Madden Grove Community of Oklahoma and spent the remainder of his working life in farming and ranching.

My Uncle Silas studied for the ministry at the Southwest Baptist Theological Seminary in Fort Worth, Texas, and was an ordained Baptist preacher. He was married to Fannie Phillips, and they had nine children. Most of Uncle Silas' adult life was spent farming in Texas and Missouri.

After the death of Aunt Laura, Uncle Joe returned to Oklahoma where he spent the remainder of his life, largely in farming.

As to the girls, they all owned farms given to them by their grandfather as wedding presents. The three of them lived all of their adult lives on their farms in the Walters and Temple areas of Oklahoma. All of the girls were married twice. Aunt Zillah, the oldest, married Robert Cowherd in 1903, and he died in 1907. They had one son, Robert Harlin Cowherd. Aunt Zillah married Charlie Thompson in 1920, and she had no children by this marriage.

Aunt Nina married Henry Phillips in 1908, and he died in 1915. They had four sons. She married James Teakel in 1923 and they had two sons

Aunt Birdie's first marriage to Leland Brown, in 1926, ended in heartbreak for her and much sadness for the family. After being married a few years, and having two daughters, Leland left and was never heard from again. It was never known whether he met with foul play or if it was a case of abandonment. Many years later, after her first husband was declared legally dead, Aunt Birdie married Olie Noblett in 1944. The Nobletts had been friends of the family for many years. There were no children by this marriage.

Like his brothers and sisters, my father was engaged in farming and ranching in his early years, although he had other business interests. This would change, however, in his later years. But I am getting ahead of the story.

II

My Early Years

I first discovered America in Plainview, Hale County, Texas, on October 26, 1920. I was one of 2,950,000 babies who came kicking and screaming into the United States that year.

I choose to be born in a year that marked a drastic political change in our nation. It was in 1920 that the Nineteenth Amendment to our Constitution enfranchised women on the same constitutional terms as men. Jack Dempsey was heavyweight boxing champion of the world, Cleveland beat out Brooklyn to win the World Series, the U. S. population stood at 106,461,000, less than one-half the 2000 census figure, and the national debt was a mere $26 billion. The debt was $8 trillion by the end of 2005. Other notable persons born in 1920 were David Brinkley, Howard Cosell, Cardinal John O'Connor, George P. Schultz, and Karol Jozef Wojtyal who on October 16, 1978, became John Paul II, the 264th pope of the Roman Catholic Church. Warren G. Harding, Republican, was elected president in November 1920 but didn't take office until March 1921.[5] The Democrat Woodrow Wilson was president the first five months of my life.

It was also in 1920 that the Eighteenth Amendment to the Constitution, which outlawed the manufacture or sale of any intoxicating liquors, went into effect, ushering in nationwide

---

[5] Prior to 1933, when the 20th constitutional amendment changed the inauguration of the President and Vice President to January, they took office in March.

prohibition. The issue of prohibition had divided the nation for years and the prohibitionists had finally succeeded in their drive to banish liquor. The Republican Party generally favored prohibition while the Democrats were divided. In the southern states, with their large protestant population, most Democrats were "dry." In the more urban northern states, with large ethnic populations, the majority was "wet." Outlawing liquor by no means put to rest the struggle between the prohibitionists and anti-prohibitionists.

I was born at home in a large two-story house located on the corner of Fourth and Beech Streets. I don't remember the details, because I was very young at the time. I have been told, however, that I was greeted by my mother and father and good ol' Doctor Gidney with much fanfare and celebration. The next day I feel certain that my sister, Hazel, who had preceded me by about five years, was overjoyed when she was introduced to her little brother who, it turned out, was to be her only brother.

In all the excitement my name came out wrong. It seems that Doctor Gidney asked my mother what she was going to name the little fellow and she replied, "I guess we'll name him after his father." Years later, when I had a need for a copy of my birth certificate, there it was— "Name: C. C. Harlin, Jr." My father had always gone by his initials, and so that is what the good doctor recorded in the birth record. He may not have known that the name was Curtis Chester. It is ironic that during the remaining years of my father's life, he went by "Curtis" and I was called "C. C." until I went into the army during World War II. Some things never change: to this day my few remaining family members (nephews and nieces, mostly) still call me C. C.

From all accounts I must have been a very active youngster. I was walking at six months, causing my mother much anxiety and fatigue. It was all she could do to keep up with my whereabouts in the large house we lived in. An example of how I constantly disrupted the household is the day when my mother, going about her usual chores, missed little C. C. She looked high and low, through all the rooms of the first floor, and I was nowhere to be found. In desperation, she went to the second floor, sure that I could not possibly have climbed the stairs. But, after searching every room, she found me in my father's upstairs study. I had emptied the contents of the wastebasket, and there I was in the overturned wastebasket. I had learned to climb stairs.

I have no recollection of the house on Beech Street, because we moved to a smaller one-story house on West Eleventh Street while I was very young. My first remembrances are at the West Eleventh Street home.

When I was about two years old, I began to have serious asthma attacks. I remember my mother holding me all night to help me get some rest. I could not run hard, like the other children, without choking up and having difficulty breathing. My asthma continued into adulthood.

In those days the medical profession did not recognize asthma as an allergic reaction. Mother would rub my chest with Vicks salve and cover it with hot flannel cloths. This was supposed to relieve me, and I guess it did to some extent. To this day, I cannot stand having greasy salve or lotion smeared on me. The doctors' advice for asthma patients was to move to other climates that were more favorable to them. Also, the doctors thought that when a person had the condition early in life they could "grow" out of it.

Another favorite remedy of my mother's was castor oil. It seems to me now that I was purged with castor oil on a frequent and routine basis. I don't remember why I was given the stuff, but I am sure my mother thought she had good reason. To make it tastier, she would mix it with freshly squeezed orange juice. This didn't improve the castor oil; it sure did ruin the orange juice. For years I could not stand to drink orange juice. With the first swallow, my taste buds would signal castor oil.

Another remedy my mother prescribed for me was one passed down to her from her mother—kerosene and sugar. This concoction was for coughs and sore throats. First, she would fill a tablespoon level full with sugar. She would then pour kerosene over the sugar until it was saturated. This semi-liquid would be swallowed to stop the cough and sooth the throat. Kerosene is probably on the current list of carcinogens, but at the time Mother used it life was uncomplicated by such concerns. Of these two remedies, I think I preferred the kerosene and sugar to the castor oil and orange juice. There is no doubt that I owe my survival to Vicks salve, castor oil, and kerosene.

The person, outside my immediate family, whom I have the earliest recollection of is Elizabeth Willis. Elizabeth was a student at Wayland College, a Baptist school located in Plainview, on out West Eleventh Street, within walking distance of where we lived. She was from a nice family that lived in the country several miles from Plainview. She lived with us and her total responsibility, in exchange for her room and board, was to look after me. She was a jewel and was like one of the family. She loved me dearly, and I loved her also. I kept in touch with her into her old age.

One of Elizabeth's routine chores was to give me my daily bath. I remember an incident that occurred one afternoon of a warm summer day. While Elizabeth was giving me my bath, I got loose from her and ran, stark naked, out the front door. I ran several laps around the house, with Elizabeth in second place, before she finally caught up with me.

We had one of those large Edison phonographs that played those thick heavy records. These records were about 12 inches in diameter with a hole in the center which was placed on a spindle in the center of a disk on the phonograph. When playing, the disk would rotate and a diamond needle would produce the sound. Elizabeth would play the current musical hits and I would listen with her, usually sitting on her lap. I loved the music. This early appreciation for music has continued throughout my life.

We also had a player piano—that mechanical monster that played paper rolls of music when someone pumped the pedals with their feet. I remember playing it when I was too small to reach the pedals from a sitting position on the bench; I would stand on the pedals and pump them by walking in place while holding on to the piano.

I was very close to my mother. She spent a lot of time with me because I was sick so often in my early years. My father did a lot of traveling when I was young and was often away from home. Also, my father was not an affectionate person. Never in my life did he tell me that he loved me, although I knew he did. Many times my mother would say to Hazel and me, "Your father loves you, he just doesn't tell you." I never saw him kiss my mother or show any sign of affection toward her. I guess it was customary for men of that period not to show their emotions as much as we do today.

The family members did love one another but did not always express it outwardly. My mother was a most kind, loving, and caring person and, in contrast to my father, always showed her affection. I am very much like her in many ways. Hazel tended to be more like our father. In our young days, people said that I favored my mother and Hazel favored her father.

My father was a rancher, the ranch being some distance from Plainview, but we always lived in town. He also owned a produce business in Plainview, with two partners, although he was not active in the day-to-day operation of the business. In those days, farmers brought their eggs, milk, cream, poultry, and other commodities to town and sold them to the produce house. The produce houses were the conduit between the producers (farmers) and the retailers. This was before large corporation farms dominated agriculture and when most farming was done by individuals and families. Produce houses played a large role in the local economies.

One of my father's partners was Dr. Z. T. Huff, dean of Wayland College. He was a close friend of the family and remained so for many years. The other partner was a man by the name of Hassel. Mr. Hassel was the manager of the business. My father was a millionaire in the days when a million dollars would buy something.

My father's main interest was the ranch and the cattle. He shipped many cattle to the markets in Kansas City and Chicago. In those days they were shipped by train. Very often he would ship an entire trainload. He would ride in the train's caboose on the trip to market, and the railroad furnished him a return ticket in a Pullman.

In those days, most of the trains that he rode on were coal-fired. The passengers had the smell of smoke in their clothes, which had a very distinctive and unpleasant odor, following a trip. I always associated this odor on my father with Kansas City. I would say he smelled like Kansas City.

When my father was gone, I would ask my mother what time he would be home. My mother, on the day he was to return, would take me to the clock and show me the position that the clock hands would be in when it was time for him to be home. One day, after we had gone through this routine, I went back to the clock and moved the hands to where my mother had indicated. I called my mother into the room, showed her the clock, and questioned why my father was not home.

In my early years, I led the life of a typical boy of that time. I played with my sister and the neighborhood children, although I was limited in how active I could be because of my asthma. I had the usual bumps and bruises and runny nose, and I looked forward every spring to the day my mother would declare it warm enough to go barefooted in the yard.

One day I was introduced to the evils of nicotine. This happened one nice summer evening when I was four or five years old, playing in the yard of one of the neighbors. The adults of the family were sitting on their front porch, enjoying the evening (before air conditioned homes) while the neighborhood children played in the yard. The man of the family finished smoking his cigarette and flipped it into the yard, still burning. I saw it and picked it up, put it in my mouth, and swaggered over to my yard where my parents were sitting on our front porch. My mother and father were horrified. My father proceeded to take me into the house and expound on the evils of smoking. He ended the lecture with the offer of a bribe (a common ploy of parents, which usually is not effective). The bribe was: If I would not smoke again before I was 21 years old, he would reward me with a sum of money, which sounded like a fortune to me at that time. I hasten to say: He did not have to pay off.

I remember the first time I heard a radio; it was in the early 1920s before I started to school. I was probably four or five years old. At that time, radios were not a common household item. One of our neighbors had purchased a new radio and was eager to show it off to his friends. The family invited our family to their home for an evening of listening.

Prior to 1920, radio broadcasting was largely experimental, with only researchers and hobbyists involved. Starting in 1920, the Westinghouse Corporation pioneered in commercial radio broadcasting with stations in Pittsburgh and Chicago. On November 2, 1920, they broadcast the presidential election returns from station KDKA in Pittsburgh. In November 1921, Westinghouse went on the air in Chicago with station KYW broadcasting the Chicago Civic Opera. The station carried the entire 1921-22 season and nothing else. It was estimated that at the start of the season there were 1,300 receivers in Chicago and at the end of the season there were 20,000. Thus, in a very short time, radio became available throughout the nation, even to small towns like Plainview, Texas.

That evening at our neighbor's home, we all gathered around the radio with great expectations. As I recall, the set consisted of a black box about two feet long and eight or nine inches high with knobs and dials on the front. The speaker, which was shaped like a deformed megaphone, sat on the top of the black box. There was also a set of headphones. I don't know why a speaker and headphones were both required, but, as it turned out, the contraption needed all the help it could get. With great fanfare, the man of the family approached the set and reverently energized it and began to manipulate the knobs, as a concertmaster would caress his violin. We were all in awe, awaiting our introduction to this miracle of the ether waves.

After much tuning and adjusting, the operator finally declared victory and cried, "There it is!" I didn't hear anything because the sound was not coming through the speaker but through the earphones. Our host passed the earphones from one person to the other, each having his or her turn. When it came my turn, all I remember hearing was a lot of cracking, hissing, and screeching, with possibly an indistinguishable voice in the background. To me it sounded more like a back-alley cat fight than entertainment. While my mother and father were polite to our hosts, they obviously concluded that radio was something our family could do without for a long time. It wasn't until the early 1930s that we had a radio in our home.

For as long as I can remember, my church has been a very important part of my life. Among my earliest recollections is going to church and Sunday school with my parents. In my first years in Plainview, I remember my mother taking me to the meetings of the Women's Missionary Union (WMU). The WMU was divided into several small groups called circles, which met in the members' homes. My mother said I was a charter member of Circle B. On Sunday mornings our family went to the First Baptist Church, which was the big church downtown affiliated with the Southern Baptist Convention. We all went to our Sunday school classes before the worship service, which started about eleven o'clock. Very often we would return for the Sunday evening service.

All of my paternal ancestors were Baptists from Samual Harlan (1778-1847), making me a fifth generation Baptist. My grandparents, on my mother's side, were also Baptists— my grandfather Dodd was a deacon. While the family for generations has been staunch Baptists, the only member of the family that I know of that was a minister of the church was my father's brother Silas.

The only automobile accident my mother ever had occurred one Sunday morning as she and I were on our way to Sunday school and church. I must have been about five years old. I don't know why Hazel and my father were not with us. A few blocks down our street there was a jog in the street. As we approached the jog I was standing on the floor on the passenger side of the front seat. The force of the turn caused me to fall sideways, and my head became lodged between the steering wheel and the dashboard. My mother was afraid to turn the wheel any further for fear of injuring my neck. At this point we were on a collision course with a large tree, which we proceeded to hit. Mother had been able to apply the brakes enough to minimize the impact; nevertheless the front bumper of our new Studebaker was severely damaged. We were both shaken up, but not seriously injured. We missed Sunday school and church that morning.

In the fall of 1927, I entered the first grade. The elementary school for our area of Plainview was located just a few blocks down our street. Of course, my mother took me the first day so I wouldn't get lost and so I could get properly enrolled. As a matter of fact, I think she took me to school and picked me up when school was over almost every day of my first term.

I guess everyone remembers their first teacher. Mine was Mrs. Mays. In my mind she was an intellectual giant (she knew everything), Florence Nightingale (she made us well when we hurt), and Saint (she could do no wrong).

One day during the morning recess, while at play in the schoolyard, I ran around the corner of the building and "wham!" I ran headlong into another student coming from the other direction. We had no way of seeing each other until we hit. We were both somewhat stunned. I had a skinned knee and, in short order, a large bump on my head. The other student had a bloody nose. Of course Mrs. Mays cleaned up our wounds and made us feel as comfortable as she could.

By the time I got home, the bump on my head was goose egg dimension and developing the color of the sky right before a bad West Texas storm. I tearfully recounted the details of my tragedy to Mother, certain that I would be an invalid the rest of my life. Mother, comforting me and hugging me, assured me that everything would be all right. In my mother's arms, I did feel secure and knew that my life had not come to a sudden and tragic end. But the thing that makes this incident still fresh in my mind is the advice she gave me. My mother said, "C. C., when you go around a corner of a building, stay wide of the building, not close to it. That way you can see anyone coming from the other side sooner, and you will have room to avoid each other." I have never forgotten that little advice. To this day, when I go around a corner of a building, I always stay away from the building and I remember my mother.

Another event that occurred in my first semester of school, which has been locked in my memory, was my first fling at show business. Near the end of the term, our school had its annual variety show. Each of the classes had an act. My class did a routine with the boys in black face (Heaven forgive us!), wearing long-tail black coats and white pants. We did some kind of song and dance. The girls in the class wore frilly dresses and did a dance routine. Then our grand finale included all of the girls and boys in one breathtaking extravaganza. I remember the boys were lined up according to height, and I was on the end because I was the smallest in the class.

We practiced for the show for weeks, and the mothers made the costumes. Most of the boys' long-tail coats were made from cheap material that had no body and did not hang well. My mother made mine out of a formal coat she got from someone, and it was elegant. I guess, as a result of this early experience, I have been somewhat of a ham, and in later years engaged in some amateur theater.

During the years we lived in Plainview, we would visit my Harlin grandparents at least once a year. The trip to Oklahoma was about 200 miles, which was not easy in the cars we had then and because of the condition of the roads. I remember the black Buick touring sedan my father had. It was sporty with the top down in the summer, but on those trips to the grandparents in the winter, it was a giant refrigerator on wheels. We would take plenty of quilts to cover with. Hazel and I would be toasty-warm in the back seat. Mother faired all right in the front passenger seat, but poor Father must have been extremely uncomfortable not being able to cover up while driving. Later my father bought a new Studebaker sedan which was much more comfortable.

My grandmother and grandfather Dodd moved to Texas sometime between 1915 and 1920. They lived on their farm in the Lelia Lake community of Donley County about 80 miles northeast of Plainview. I remember this being a very sandy area. The greatest danger in driving in the area was getting stuck in the sand. Only a few of the major roads were paved. On the unpaved roads, like the one to my grandparents' home, the driver would not dare leave the main tracks unless it was absolutely necessary. It was especially difficult when two cars met and one had to pull over to the side of the road. Very often the unfortunate driver would find his car wheels hub-deep in the sand. The more throttle he would give the engine, the faster the wheels would turn, and the deeper they would dig into the sand.

When we traveled to our grandparents for Christmas, Mother would have a difficult time hiding our presents in the crowded car. Cars in those days did not have luggage space like those of today. The Buick touring sedan had only the front and back seat areas. Everything had to go in there. Several times, Hazel and I had previews of what "Santa Claus" was going to bring us.

One of the big thrills in going to and returning from Oklahoma was going down and up the Cap Rock. This is an escarpment which separates the High Plains from the Central Lowland of north-central Texas. The High Plains is as flat as a table top, except for the many playas, or "Buffalo Wallows," as they were called locally, that dotted the area. Leaving the High Plains at about the town of Matador, we would descend through a rough and rocky region of outcrops several hundred feet within a short distance. Having lived all of my life in the flat, treeless expanse of the High Plains, this experience was like driving through the Grand Canyon. On our return trips we had to ascend the Cap Rock. This was a real endurance test for the car. If she were inclined to run hot, climbing the Cap Rock would assuredly blow her radiator cap.

A common problem of early-day automobile travel was the car's engine overheating. When this happened, steam would shoot from the radiator and the only thing to do was to stop and hope there was a water source nearby. Many drivers carried a bucket in their car to get water when the engine overheated.

A major challenge of traveling by car in those days was the inevitable flat tire. People who drove expected to have a number of flats if they traveled very far. We had our share on our trips. Car owners were prepared for this inconvenience. Every car was equipped with a jack, tire tool, lug wrench, air pump, and tire patching kit. Those were the days before tubeless tires. If the flat was due to a nail or thorn or some other sharp object's making a small hole in the tube, the repair could usually be made by putting a "cold patch" over the hole. Cold patches were thin precut rubber pieces of

29

assorted sizes, which were stuck on the tire tube, over the hole, with special rubber cement. Sometimes they did the job, other times they would come off after a few miles of driving. More serious tire troubles, such as blowouts or large holes in tubes or tires, which were common, required the services of a garage.

The cars of the 1920s provided much faster means of transportation than the horse and buggy, but sometimes they were lacking in reliability.

I remember one very special trip to Oklahoma. In August 1928, my grandmother and grandfather Harlin celebrated their golden wedding anniversary. All of their seven children and their families were there. According to a newspaper account of the event, 21 grandchildren were present. There were also other relatives and many friends. I remember being with my cousins, several of them about my age. It was exciting to explore the upstairs of the house and the barn and other out-buildings. My grandfather plowed his land by horsepower, as did most other farmers of that time. He had a beautiful matched team of Percheron horses. They were a real marvel for a town boy to see.

My favorite uncle was my father's brother Joe. Uncle Joe lived near Mustang, Oklahoma, which is near Oklahoma City. Several times during my early years we visited him. He had a large family and two of his sons were near my age. Uncle Joe was a farmer and I loved to visit there. He had an apple orchard, and it seemed that we were often there during apple-picking time. He had a cider press, and I remember drinking the fresh apple juice right from the press.

On one of our visits, Uncle Joe gave my mother a bushel of apples for canning. After we got home, it was a few days before Mother got around to the apples. One day a neighborhood lady called my mother and asked her if she knew that I was selling apples, door-to-door. Of course it was a surprise to my mother. I had decided to go into business for myself. I don't think I actually sold any of the apples because, as I remember, the lady who "snitched" on me was one of the first ones I called on. Nevertheless, my first business venture ended in failure.

Uncle Joe was a great taffy candy maker. When we visited him, Hazel and I always asked him to make taffy. He would make a big batch for us, pulling the very hot candy with his bare hands to the right consistency. Years later, when I had children of my own, he visited us and once again made taffy for us.

My tenure in the Plainview public school system was short-lived. During the mid-term break of my first year, our family moved to a farm in Donley County, northeast of Plainview. I was too young at the time to grasp what had happened, but there was to be a drastic change in the family's economic status and standard of living.

III

The Lean Years

Most people know about the Great Depression of the 1930s, which was inaugurated by the stock market crash of 1929. Through the study of history, hearing it from parents and relatives, or by actually having lived during those times, we know the consequences of the Depression. Fortunes were wiped out over night, homes were lost, and once financially well-off families were reduced to poverty.

The cause of the Great Depression has been attributed to many things. Since it was a worldwide phenomenon, most businessmen and government leaders blamed it on events outside their countries. The socialist, Ramsey MacDonald, who was Prime Minister of Great Britain, blamed capitalism. He said capitalism had broken down everywhere. The Germans claimed that the harsh terms of the Versailles Treaty, which ended World War I, was the cause. France blamed the monetary policies of Great Britain and the United States for "exporting unemployment" by substituting machines for workers. In the United States, most Americans, as well as foreigners, put the blame on the stock market crash of October 1929.[6]

Regardless of the cause, the depression, in short order, brought disastrous results. Financial institutions collapsed. Over 1,300 banks failed by the end of 1930, with nearly an additional 2,300 failures during 1931.[7] Worldwide unemployment was at an all-time high. Unemployment in the

---

[6] John A. Garraty, *The Great Depression*, p. 5.

[7] *Ibid.*, pp. 34-35.

United States has been estimated at 25 percent of the civilian labor force at its peak in 1933.[8] "In the United States, where unemployment was extremely high, the absence of any national system of unemployment insurance or welfare when the Depression began made solving the problem especially difficult. The long American experience of more or less automatic economic expansion made adjusting to Depression conditions harder still for many unemployed people."[9]

What is not so commonly known of is the "Agricultural Depression," which preceded the 1929 crash. In fact, there has been considerable debate as to whether or not the real cause of the Great Depression was actually the depressed state of agriculture.

Garraty relates the agricultural depression to World War I.[10] World War I caused food production in Europe to decline and encouraged farmers in other countries, including the United States, to increase production of grains and livestock. With the end of the war, European countries resumed agricultural production, and in the United States agriculture continued to expand, assisted by new mechanization, resulting in world surpluses in the 1920s. Consequently, prices for agricultural products fell to disastrous levels. The combined average price of leading agricultural commodities fell about 30 percent between 1925 and 1929.[11] From 1919 to 1921 the average price received by farmers and ranchers for beef cattle dropped almost 50 percent.[12] These low prices continued through the 1920s. My father was a victim of this debacle, and he never recovered financially.

---

[8] United States Department of Commerce, *Historical Statistics of the United States 1975*, Part I, p.26.

[9] John A. Garraty, *The Great Depression*, p. 124.

[10] *Ibid.*, pp. 52-53.

[11] *Ibid.*, pp. 53-54.

[12] United States Department of Commerce, *Historical Statistics of the United States, Part I*, p.457.

In those years, as stated earlier, my father dealt in large numbers of beef cattle. He not only raised cattle on his ranch, he bought cattle for resale from other producers. He was shipping thousands of cattle each year to the markets in Kansas City and Chicago in trainload lots. Then the bottom dropped out. My father told me that the market dropped so rapidly that the last loads of cattle he shipped decreased so much in value, *while in transit*, that their sale price would not pay for their freight!

By the fall of 1927, my father's financial condition had deteriorated almost to the point of bankruptcy. He salvaged enough from the ranch to acquire a small farm in Donnely County to which we moved in December 1927.

I started to school at the beginning of the second half of my first grade in a two-room schoolhouse located about two miles from where we lived. The name of the school was Windy Valley. Hazel and I were in separate rooms, she being four or five grades ahead of me. I remember Hazel and I walked to and from school except when the weather was very bad.

This school was quite different from the school in Plainview. The most obvious difference was that children of different ages were in the same room, and the teacher divided her time between the different grades. The classes that she was not working with at any given time were supposed to be doing assigned work. This made it hard for the children to concentrate on their assignments, and most of us were not very productive during those periods.

Another difference was the nature of the plumbing system. The restrooms were separate, detached structures, commonly called outhouses or privies. There was one for boys and one for girls. The boys' was a four- or five-holer, as I recall. I assume the girls' was similarly equipped. The water supply system consisted of a hand pump located on a direct line between the outhouses and the schoolhouse. I suppose this location was by design in order to reduce travel time while going to and from the restroom and getting a drink of water. These two operations were usually accomplished on the same outing.

The highlight of my semester at Windy Valley was winning the class spelling bee at the end of school. As champion, I was presented a prize by the teacher. For the life of me I don't remember exactly what it was. I think it might have been a book. When I arrived home and displayed my prize to my parents, Mother asked the inevitable mother-question, "What did you say to the teacher?" "Much obliged," I responded. Mother expressed her disapproval (the acceptable answer was "Thank you.") But in later years she admitted she thought it was cute.

The time we lived in the Windy Valley community was not easy. My father worked the land, terracing the sloping, highly eroded fields with a homemade, horse drawn implement. I do not recall what his crops were, but he worked very hard. Our house was nice by standards of the day for farm residences but not as nice as our home in Plainview. Like the school I attended, it had outdoor plumbing and well water. Being before the days of rural electrification, we used kerosene lamps for light and wood or coal stoves for cooking and heating. We had chickens and milk cows which helped supply our needs. I adjusted to the life of a farm boy very well; my recollection of the time is not unpleasant. I am sure, though, the time was fraught with worry for my mother and father.

Times were tough all over. Farm prices were low and, by the end of the summer, my father had to give up on the farm. We moved in with my mother's parents who lived on a farm near Lelia Lake, also in Donnley County, not very far from where we had lived. Hazel and I were enrolled in the Lelia Lake School at the start of the school year.

My grandparents' house was rather full after the four of us moved in. In addition to my grandparents, my Uncle Wylie Towery, his daughter Wynon, and his son Lovell also lived there. Uncle Wylie was the husband of my mother's only sister, Clennie, who died when Wynon was just a baby. Uncle Wylie and his two children had lived with my grandparents after Aunt Clennie's death. He was a barber by trade and did not always live with the Dodds, but my grandmother and grandfather had taken the responsibility of raising his children.

During the last few months we lived with my grandparents, Uncle Lloyd, mother's only brother, and his wife and baby boy also moved in. It was not uncommon during those years for families to move in with each other, for those were difficult times. However, we were not there very long after they came.

My cousin Wynon was about three years older than I. Lovell was several years older than she, probably 18 or 19 years old the year we lived there. He was not in school and "bummed" around, looking for work, as many young men did at that time. His primary mode of transportation was by freight train—riding the rods they called it. When he returned from his trips, he often had some wild stories to tell.

All of the men, except my grandfather, were gone much of the time looking for work or working at whatever job they could find. I remember my father being gone on job-hunting expeditions. One time he needed a recent picture of himself for some job applications. The expenditure of their meager funds for that purpose was a major decision for my parents.

My grandfather raised cotton and corn. He also had a big watermelon patch. I remember in the summer we would burst a big melon in the field and eat the choice heart meat. During very hot days, we would pick a melon early in the morning and put it in the well house so it would be cool when we ate it later in the day. They were delicious and there were plenty of them. During cotton-picking time, all of the men picked cotton, not only in my grandfather's field, but also for some of the neighbors.

My cousin Lovell was a natural-born clown. He was always joking and pulling pranks. I remember one time he made some extremely tall stilts. They must have been eight or nine feet off the ground. They were so tall he would have to climb up on the garage to get on them. He would walk around in the yard and, of course, we smaller children thought it was great fun. My grandmother almost had a nervous breakdown over it; she was afraid he would fall on one of us.

One day he walked to Lelia Lake, which was probably about a mile away, on his stilts. Lelia Lake was a very small, one-street town, and most of the stores had wooden awnings over the sidewalks, which was then common. Lovell walked up and down the street and, from time to time, would sit down on a store awning to rest, attracting a lot of attention. That was probably one of the most exciting days in the history of Lelia Lake.

I remember Lovell telling about how he would sometimes eat when he was on the road. Money was scarce and very often he didn't have enough for a meal. Well, as he told it, he would go into a restaurant and order a bowl of soup. He would eat it almost to the bottom of the bowl and then place a fly, which he had caught and brought with him, in the remaining soup. He would call the proprietor and express his outrage that the establishment would allow such unsanitary conditions. This would attract the attention of other customers and the poor proprietor would gladly forfeit the payment for the soup to get him out of his restaurant. I guess we can become quite ingenious when we are hungry and without money.

I don't remember very much about my second grade in the Lelia Lake School. We didn't live very far from the school, probably about a mile. Hazel, Wynon, and I walked to and from school. I do remember having a rather difficult time with my schoolwork. My mother would help me with my lessons at night. I was bothered a lot with asthma, which made it hard to concentrate on my studies. I still have the picture in my mind of my mother and me sitting at a table, lighted by a kerosene lamp, she patiently trying to help me prepare for the next day, and my gasping for breath because of my asthmatic condition. Many nights my mother would put me to bed with my sobbing in frustration over my lessons.

Although times were very hard, looking back on that year it seemed to be a happy time, at least for us children. Hazel and I enjoyed being with Wynon, and we became quite close. While the adults had many worries, I don't think they ever lost their sense of humor. I don't remember any ringing of hands or lamenting our plight, but I do remember lots of laughter and fun and good humor.

By the time school was out that year, my parents had decided that we would move to south Texas. My father had visited the hill country around Kerrville, Texas, on one of his trips. It was a health resort area and many people with tuberculosis and respiratory diseases moved there for their health. The primary reason for moving to that area was the hope that the climate would relieve my asthma. So, in the spring of 1929, we moved, with all of us and our belongings in a borrowed truck, to a rented house located a few miles south of Kerrville.

The house we lived in that first summer was located on a farm. We just rented the house, not the land. I don't remember very much about the house except it had a big screened front porch where Hazel and I slept during the hot nights. The house was located on the main highway between Kerrville and San Antonio.

A small creek flowed through the property about 100 yards from the house. The highway bridge, which crossed the creek, had been washed out by a recent flood and was being rebuilt. My father got a job with the highway department on the bridge project.

The washed-out bridge was almost my undoing. Although there were barricades and lanterns on both sides of the creek to warn motorists, many nights cars would hit the barricades and even wind up in the creek. Warning lights and signals were not as effective then as they are now. Many nights the wind would blow out the kerosene lanterns leaving the scene in total darkness. When this happened, the drivers had no advance warning of the hazard ahead. We would hear the crash of the cars into the barricades; my father would go out to see what help he could give. A few times there were serious injuries. When the accidents happened—and they happened several times almost every week—our family would be awake most of the night. This had a serious effect on our family. I was especially distressed by it. In a short time I became extremely nervous and could not sleep at nights. This went on all summer.

My father also worked at a dairy that was located near the farm we lived on. He would get up early to help with the morning milking and then work on the bridge project all day. Then he would return to the dairy to help with the evening chores. Those were long days for my father, but during those times one had to do what one could to make ends meet.

In spite of the sleepless nights, it was an enjoyable summer for me. The area around Kerrville was very different from the flat treeless plains of the Texas Panhandle. The hilly terrain was covered with native trees and vegetation and there were many small streams that flowed into the majestic Guadeloupe River, which traversed the region. The house we lived in was within walking distance of the Guadeloupe. My father and I often fished there, which was a new experience for me. The abundant wildlife, which included deer, wild turkey, and squirrels, was a delight for the whole family.

At the end of the summer, we moved into a rented house in Kerrville, located on Jefferson Street, across the street from the First Baptist Church. Hazel and I started to school, once again, in new schools. I was in the third grade and this was the fourth school I had attended. Hazel was in junior high school. The elementary school and the junior high school were across the street from each other and within easy walking distance of our house.

Kerrville is located on the banks of the Guadeloupe River, about 65 miles northwest of San Antonio. It was the center of a health and recreational resort area. A large veteran's tuberculosis hospital, Legion Hospital, was located there as well as several private sanatoriums.

Several summer camps for boys and girls were located in the area, primarily on the river upstream from Kerrville. Camps Stewart, Mystic, and Waldemar, to name a few, were quite expensive and attracted boys and girls of wealthy families from all over, many coming from Houston and San Antonio. There were other facilities for families.

Many homes in the area were occupied by families only during the summer. Kerrville, located in the hill country, was much cooler than many parts of Texas. The elevation increased about 1,000 feet, in the 65 miles from San Antonio to Kerrville. Humidity was low, and the abundance of trees provided ample shade. Because of the favorable climate, people would spend their summers there to avoid the heat of their permanent homes.

The population of Kerrville, when we first moved there, was about 5,000. During the summer, however, the number of people in Kerrville and the immediate area probably doubled. The town was quite lively then, with all the social and recreational activities.

The economy of Kerrville was service and retail oriented. Kerrville was the largest town between San Antonio and San Angelo and drew on quite a large trade territory. The agriculture of the region was predominantly sheep and Angora goat ranching.

Although the first few years we were in the area were the worst of the Depression, conditions in Kerrville were not too bad, compared to other parts of the country. Many of the permanent residents of Kerrville were World War I veterans, on pensions, who had been attracted to the area for health reasons. Many had come, as patients, to Legion Hospital and had stayed in the area. The area was also home for many wealthy retirees who had moved there at the end of their careers because of the climate. So, there was a sizable base population with steady incomes, even during the Depression.

Kerrville had no manufacturing; consequently, there was no unemployment due to plant shutdowns, as in industrial areas. While business was slow, employment remained fairly even. Even so, jobs were not easy to find and my father had difficulty meeting our minimum needs. Looking back, I wonder how we got along as well as we did. To my knowledge, our family never received any aid from the government or any other source. At least we had a roof over our heads, clothes on our backs, and food on our table. It was said that Kerrville was a wonderful place to live, but no one should move there unless they had plenty of money to start with.

The business community was dominated by a few old established families. Foremost among them were the Schreiners. Captain Charles Schreiner was an early settler of the area. At the time we moved there he had passed on, but several of his sons lived in beautiful homes and were very influential in business. One of the two banks in Kerrville was the Schreiner Bank; one of the then few remaining privately owned banks in the country. Schreiner Department Store dominated almost a whole block of downtown Kerrville. The Schreiners also operated a large wool and mohair warehouse through which much of the wool and mohair of the area was traded. They also had extensive land holdings around Kerrville.

Other influential business leaders were the Petersons, the Faucetts, and the Pampells. Major landmarks on Water Street, the main street of Kerrville, were the Schreiner Bank,

Schreiner Department Store, Faucetts Furniture Store, Pampells Drug Store, Petersons General Motors Dealership, and the Bluebonnet Hotel.

During the first year we lived in Kerrville, my father worked at several jobs. At first he continued to work for the Highway Department. Then he got involved in cutting cedar posts. The area contained many native cedar trees, and posts cut from them were the preferred posts for fences. This was before the chain saw, and the trees were cut down by hand using hand axes. Once a tree was felled, it was cut into posts of varying diameters and sorted according to size. Posts were then loaded onto trucks by hand labor and hauled to market. This was hard work, and the pay depended on the number of posts cut. The post cutters of the area occupied the bottom rung of the social ladder, but it did put food on our table.

I didn't do well that year in the third grade. Except for the first half of the first grade, my prior schooling generally had been in rural schools, which did not prepare me very well for a progressive school like Kerrville had. At the end of the school year I was not passed to the fourth grade, which meant I had to repeat the last semester of the third grade.

I was not accepted very well by my third grade peers. The role of a newcomer is never easy, but I was a poor newcomer thrust into a fairly well-to-do group, most of whom had been together all of their lives. I was an outsider with nothing special to offer the class. I was pretty much left alone and I don't remember having any close friends. I am sure that my unhappiness that year contributed to my poor performance.

The most enjoyable part of that year was my pets. I don't remember how I acquired one of them, but I had a very large, solid black rabbit. I also had several wild rabbits, which my father or I caught in the woods. I got one of them, a cottontail, when it was very small, and it grew to adulthood. My mother was very tolerant of my menagerie and let me keep my pets in the house. The cottontail grew up with the big black rabbit, and they were inseparable. They were always together as they hopped around the house. I also had white rats and mice, guinea pigs, and squirrels, at various times.

After living in Kerrville a year, we moved to Center Point, a town of just a few hundred people, 10 miles southeast of Kerrville. I don't know anything about the circumstances of our move, but I am sure they were economic.

Sometime before our move, Grandfather and Grandmother Dodd had moved to Center Point. We moved into a house that was the second house from my grandparents. The Harlesses, an elderly couple, lived between us. I believe they owned the houses my grandparents and our family lived in.

Our house was not in the same class as the one we lived in in Kerrville. It was comfortable enough and had a large fenced yard, but it did not have indoor plumbing. The Harlesses were a very nice old couple and I helped them with their chores. During the winter I kept the wood box on their back porch filled. They paid me 50 cents a week. That was big money for me and probably the first I had ever earned.

Once again, Wynon, Hazel, and I were together. Lovell was then on his own and no longer living with his grandparents. Uncle Wylie was living with them and the responsibility of taking care of my grandparents was mostly his. My grandfather was in very poor health. During the winter his condition worsened, and he died March 4, 1931. He was buried in the Center Point cemetery.

During the summer months, my father and Uncle Wylie had a large tomato patch of several acres. It was very productive and they packed the tomatoes in crates and sold them at the market in San Antonio. Uncle Wylie had an old enclosed truck of some kind that they used. After the tomato season was over, they bought produce on the San Antonio market and sold it to stores, mostly in Kerrville.

When I started to school that fall in Center Point, because of the difference in their system, I was placed in the fourth grade. I would have repeated the second half of the third grade, had I still been in Kerrville. Unlike my experience in Kerrville, I seemed to fit in with my classmates and soon made friends.

One of my prized possessions in Center Point was a large Toggenburg goat. I bought him from one of my new friends for 50 cents. He ran loose in the back yard and became very protective of his territory. You had to keep a close eye on him; you could never turn your back on him. When he caught you not looking he would lower his head and charge; the next thing you knew, you could be picking yourself up off of the ground. He was no respecter of persons. My mother and Hazel both had encounters with him.

He was a natural-born pugilist. I would tease him and he would rare up on his hind legs and come at me just like a prizefighter. I also improvised a set of harnesses and would hitch him to my wagon. I finally became tired of him and traded him to another of my friends for a baseball glove and 50 cents. The baseball glove was clear profit.

During the summer that we moved to Center Point, Hazel worked in a grocery store in Kerrville. I guess she got the job through our father's contacts in selling produce to the stores. While working in Kerrville she met a young man by the name of Henry Covert, who became very important in her life. They were married a couple of years later.

During that summer there was a record flood on the Guadeloupe River. At the time, Hazel was in Kerrville and my father was somewhere between San Antonio and Kerrville with a load of produce. Mother and I were in Center Point. The high bridge from the main highway into Center Point washed out and the low-water bridge into town was inundated; we were isolated from the world. Our family of four was scattered in three directions, unable to communicate with each other. I recall Mother's and my walking to the river one day and seeing a large crowd of people on the opposite side, among them was my father. He was unable to get across, but we waved and he went on to Kerrville. After a few days the water receded, and we were once again able to be together.

According to my memory, the time that we lived in Center Point, 1930-31, was the worst time, financially, for our family. Because of my father's dealing in produce, we had something to eat, but cash was very scarce. When Christmas approached, the biggest item was Hazel's present to Henry. The Coverts owned and operated a dairy in Kerrville and by our standards were fairly well off, financially. Hazel wanted her present to be something nice but there was not much money to spend. She finally decided on a silk scarf.

I remember Christmas morning. I had fruit in my stocking— we always had fruit in the house that Daddy would bring home from the market. My one and only present was a small dictionary, which I needed for school. My mother was heartbroken because they were not able to give any more; the money was just not there. As long as my mother lived, anytime anyone spoke of that Christmas tears would come to her eyes.

In my early years I always went to Vacation Bible School. It was usually held two or three weeks after school was out for the summer. This is one institution that has apparently withstood the test of time, although I am not acquainted with what is taught today. In my time, we would sing, learn scripture verses, have a time for creative handy work, and always have a period of worship. Usually, the worship period was conducted by the pastor, or educational director, or some other staff member. The emphasis during these periods was on "being saved." Some kind of "invitation" was usually extended, at least toward the end of the school. Very often the invitation would consist of a series of leading questions which seemed to be designed to scare the children into, "...accepting Jesus as your personal savior."

I am certainly not against trying to direct our children toward the Christian life, in fact I encourage it. But in retrospect, the tactics used in those sessions appeared to put an awful lot of pressure on the young and innocent. All that was necessary was for one child to "come forward" and there would immediately be a stampede of like minded "sinners" surging forward. I know of what I speak—I was one who was caught up in this. I do not know exactly how old I was at the time, but I "went forward" during one of these highly emotional services. I would guess I was around eight or ten years old.

Before school started the next year, we moved back to Kerrville into a rented house on Robinson Street. I started to school that fall in the fifth grade. My father had acquired a truck, and once again he was cutting cedar posts. This time he not only cut the posts but he hauled them to market in his own truck, realizing more money for his labor than previously.

This time I was better accepted by my classmates than when we first lived in Kerrville. I made friends and slowly became adjusted. Our family also began to make friends, some of whom would endure for years to come. The romance between Hazel and Henry continued to blossom.

At that time my mother and father were very protective of me. In those days, crime was not a problem, especially in small towns like Kerrville. No one locked their doors, people left the keys in their cars, and no one feared to walk anywhere, day or night. I was shielded, not because of fear for my safety, but for fear of moral corruption.

I remember coming home one day excited over the prospect of selling newspapers. A friend of mine sold papers on the street downtown, and I had a chance to do the same. When I presented the proposition to my parents, I was told that they didn't think it was a good idea. It soon came out that the reason they objected was that they were afraid I would hear bad words and pick up bad habits if exposed to the people on the streets.

Another time I had a chance to work at the local bottling plant. My parents had the same objections and also thought the work would be too hard for me. So, while other boys of my age were able to pick up a little money doing small jobs, I could do nothing to put money in my pocket.

At this point in my life there is nothing to be gained by trying to place blame, but the early attitude of my parents probably had a negative effect on my personality. I feel their lack of encouragement may have contributed to a lack of confidence, especially in my early years. I am sure they thought they were doing what was best for me, though.

The second year after moving back to Kerrville, a new grocery store was opened downtown by two brothers named Neeley. My father was hired to help set up the store and worked there after it opened for two or three years. Neither one of the Neeley brothers had had any experience in the grocery business; my father pretty much managed the business.

Sometime in 1932 or 1933 we moved to another rental house on Sidney Baker Street. The house was on a large lot. In addition, a large vacant lot next to the house was included. The vacant lot became an improvised park for baseball, croquet, kite flying and other activities of the neighborhood children.

I remember taking an agriculture course in school which required having a project. My project was two lambs. Having the large vacant lot, which was fenced, gave them plenty of room to graze. There are probably not any towns today, even small ones, that would allow any livestock to be kept within their limits. All of the students were encouraged to show their animals at the Kerr County Fair in the spring. They were judged and could be sold through the auction at the conclusion of the fair. I didn't win any ribbons, but I did sell my lambs at the auction. I doubt that they brought enough to pay for their feed.

We always had dogs when I was growing up. During the years on Sidney Baker Street, our dog was Buster, an Alaskan Spitz. He was a beautiful animal and the whole family loved him dearly. He was very smart and easy to train. His primary chore was bringing in the newspaper every morning. Early each morning he would go out and wait for the paper to be thrown into the front yard. He would bring it to the front door and scratch on the screen until someone came to let him bring it in.

Those were the days before leash laws, and ol' Buster could be seen roaming our part of town. Everyone knew him and respected him. One day he didn't come home. After searching the neighborhood, we found him: he had apparently been hit by a car. His death was a real loss to the entire family.

Sometime later, Daddy brought home a female dog which he had found beside the road, almost dead. She was small, of mixed ancestry, and in terrible condition. She obviously had not had any care for days and was on the verge of starvation. With tender loving care, we soon nursed her back to health and were surprised to see that she was in a "family way." Soon she delivered her litter, which consisted of only one little male pup. His mother did not live very long, but we kept the pup for several years. We named him Scraps.

During those years, I finally began to earn a little money from jobs that were acceptable to my parents. First, I delivered circulars door-to-door for some businesses in town. In those days, that was a common way for businesses to advertise sales and other promotions. I would earn maybe a couple of dollars for a half-day to a full day of work. Then I got a route selling magazines—*Ladies Home Journal*, *Saturday Evening Post*, and *Country Gentleman*. I did very well and was able to add to my customers regularly. I had no transportation, so I walked, carrying my magazines in a canvas bag slung over my shoulder.

My first big purchase was in the early 1930s when I bought my first bicycle. I remember it well: it was a beautiful new blue and white, 28-inch, Western Flyer. I bought it at Mr. Couch's bicycle shop for $25. I made a deal with Mr. Couch to pay five dollars a month. There was no paperwork, no co-signing, nothing complicated, just our understanding that I would make my monthly payments. I remember the pride I felt each month when I went to the shop to make my payment. I always had the money and was never late.

With my new transportation, I expanded my business. I began distributing the *Grit*, a weekly newspaper, published in Pennsylvania, I think. While the newspaper did not have wide circulation, those who subscribed to it were extremely loyal. I picked up the *Grit* route from someone who had to give it up. I received the bundle of papers by mail every week and delivered them on my bicycle. I was fairly successful at adding subscribers. With my magazine route, my newspaper route, and picking up jobs delivering circulars, I was doing quite well, thank you.

In the spring of 1933, Hazel graduated from Tivy High School in Kerrville. The next year, on June 9, 1934, she and Henry were married. They had a very nice wedding in our home. The living room, the scene of the wedding, was elaborately decorated with many flowers. The ring bearer and flower girl were a nephew and niece of Henry's. Our pastor, Reverend Smith, performed the ceremony.

A few days before the wedding, I came down with a bad case of chicken pox. This turn of events cast a dark cloud of uncertainty over the wedding plans. There was not so much concern for the invited guests and the adult members of the wedding party, but what about the three- and four-year-old ring bearer and flower girl who had not had chicken pox? After consultation with the doctor, and with agreement of the children's parents, it was decided to proceed with the wedding, as planned. There was one change though: I would not be permitted to attend. When the big day arrived, as the ceremony proceeded in the living room, I remained in the kitchen. From the kitchen door, I could see through the dining room into the living room, so that I did see my sister married, from a distance, standing in my pajamas.

In 1935, my father left his job at Neeley's grocery store to open his own business. He rented a building on Water Street, which had formerly been a movie theater. He remodeled the front of the building for the store, Dixie Market (the theater had been named Dixie Theater), and had plenty of room in the back for storage. The specialty of the store was fresh fruits and vegetables, but other grocery items were stocked. From the day it opened, I worked in the store after school and during the summers and on weekends.

In my youth, the family continued to go to church fairly regularly. There were times during the lean years of the Depression that my father stayed home because he didn't feel that he had proper clothes to wear, but my mother, Hazel, and I usually went. It is sad that the one institution, the church, which is supposed to welcome all people, can make the unfortunate feel so unwelcome. These same unfortunate people are usually in great need of the ministry which the church allegedly provides. I say the church, but the church is people. The people are the culprits, and few of us are without blame.

In those days the Baptist Church had a youth organization, the Baptist Young Peoples Union (BYPU), which met Sunday evenings before the evening worship service. As a teenager, I was active in this group. It was a mixed group, which made it more interesting and inviting than Sunday school which was segregated by sex, boys and girls going to different classes. I cannot remember anything very spiritually uplifting coming from these meetings, but they did offer an opportunity for the boys and girls to fraternize. Some of the activities between the sexes, before and after these meetings, were a far cry from those promoted by the church.

My days in high school were filled with all sorts of experiences, both good and bad. I developed close friendships, established myself with my peers, and pursued a variety of activities. I was not a good student. Later experiences proved that my poor grades were not because of a lack of intelligence, but due to a lack of interest and the fact that I did not apply myself.

My best friend was Arlton Hatch. We were the same age and in the same grade in school. He was an only child and his parents lived on a ranch some distance west of Kerrville. There was no high school near their ranch and so he came to Kerrville to go to school. I don't know how it was arranged, but Arlton came to live with us during his years in high school. We did everything together; we were like brothers. He was a much more serious student than I; he always found time to study. I was probably a bad influence on him.

My main concern in those years was having a good time. If school did not interfere with my other activities, I would take care of schoolwork. Otherwise, school was not a high priority. Of course my parents were interested in my education, but they did not push me. In fact, parental encouragement was minimal. They didn't instill in me the necessity of applying myself to my studies and the importance of a good education. I had the feeling that they didn't really expect much from me, and I didn't intend to surprise them. So, I muddled through, just barely passing from one grade to the next.

The only subjects that I did well in were history and civics. I enjoyed those classes and always made good grades in them with little effort. I remember the semester we studied the United States Constitution in civics class. I became completely immersed in it. At the end of the semester I was the only student in the class who made a perfect score on the final examination. I was Miss Harriett Garrett's star pupil. She really made me feel good by calling my accomplishment to the attention of the principal and the other teachers. My

51

other teachers probably thought that there had been a mistake, based on my performance in their classes.

Mathematics was my poorest area. I always scored just high enough to barely pass to the next level. When I graduated, I graduated "conditionally" in mathematics. That meant that I squeaked by in high school, but my mathematics credits were not transferable to college. I was never good in foreign languages either. I took three years of Spanish in high school. However, all three years were in Spanish I. I think the teacher enjoyed my company so much that she kept me in her class year after year.

Football was big in Kerrville then, as it still is in all of Texas. The year 1936 was outstanding for Tivy High School's football team. It was one of those teams that coaches dream of. It was made up largely of boys who had grown up and played football together since grade school. They had no trouble winning the district, quarterfinals, semifinals, and were matched with Amarillo High School, a much larger school, for the state championship.

A train trip was organized to take the Kerrville fans to Amarillo for the game. My father and I went on the train. It was one big celebration the entire trip. But alas, Amarillo proved to be too much for us. Although we gave a good account of ourselves—the score was fairly close as I remember—Tivy High lost the game. While we were all disappointed, the town had a great feeling of pride. Tivy had never gone so far in the playoffs before.

Many players on the 1936 team were seniors and most of them received scholarships from colleges. Some did extremely well on college teams. The Kerrville Junior Chamber of Commerce collected money and presented Tivy High School Coach Hillard with a new automobile. That was truly a glorious year for Tivy High School and Kerrville.

Sunday school always held a high priority with me, in my early years as a student and later as a teacher. I recall two of my Sunday school teachers during my junior and high school years in Kerrville—Gordon Rayford, who was a barber, and Eugene Butt, who worked at the post office. Looking back, I greatly appreciate their influence on my life. They were both gentle and kind men who were truly interested in the spiritual well-being of their class members. I am sure there were many times when they felt they were wasting their time on us, because we often showed little interest in what was being said. But, at least in my case, I learned much from those Sunday morning sessions, although it probably was not apparent at the time.

During my junior year in high school I had a real conversion experience during a revival meeting in our church. The preacher for this meeting was Dr. Tidwell who, at the time, was the president of Baylor University. He was not like so many of the other visiting revival preachers that I had heard. He was very calm and dignified and it seemed more like he was having a personal conversation with you than preaching.

A few years earlier, as I previously mentioned, I "went forward" during one of those emotional services and was baptized. This time it was different. The way the preacher presented the questions of sin and salvation and our need for God in our life was so clear. In one of the services, I truly realized my sinful condition and felt a real need to accept Jesus as my savior. In a very reasoned and unemotional way I presented myself during the invitation. I was baptized again at the age of sixteen.

After high school graduation, whether I was working, in college, or in the Army, I always attended church services regularly. Even being out from under the influence of my parents, I still felt a need to be involved in worship services. The early teachings and examples of my parents and others, such as Mr. Rayford and Mr. Butt, were indelibly imprinted in my value system.

In my early high school days, probably in my freshman year, I started taking drum lessons from Mr. Ruben Hartman. In those days, most towns, even the small ones, had a town band. Mr. Hartman was the director of the Kerrville band. It didn't take me long to learn enough to start playing snare drum with the band. The band gave weekly concerts on the courthouse lawn during the summer, and played for special occasions such as parades, fairs, etc at other times. I soon became bored with the drums and, because Mr. Hartman had an old trombone I could use, I switched to the trombone. I don't know how much the lessons cost, but Mr. Hartman took his pay in groceries from our store.

I liked the trombone and did very well. I will never forget a story Mr. Hartman would tell me nearly every week when I went for my lesson. He would tell about him giving Jack Teagarden his first trombone lessons when he lived in Vernon, Texas. By that time Teagarden was one of the top musicians in jazz and swing circles, then playing with Paul Whiteman's Orchestra. Mr. Hartman would always end by saying, "...and you know, today Jack Teagarden is making $150 a week." That was big money in those days. I guess that was an inspiration for me. I have always felt a close kinship with Jack Teagarden, being trombone brothers, having had the same musical father.

In my junior year in high school, another music teacher moved to Kerrville. His name was Stan Thal. Before that time Tivy High School had no band and no instrumental music program. Mr. Thal offered private lessons and made an attempt at organizing the first high school band. In addition, to supplement his meager income, he organized a dance band. Kerrville had had a dance band before, headed by Bobby Schmerbeck and his brother, but it had disbanded about the time Thal moved to town. Thal invited me to play trombone. I became a professional musician at the age of sixteen.

Those were the early days of the "Big Band" era and swing was the craze. The bands of Glen Miller, Benny Goodman, Jimmy and Tommy Dorsey, Count Basie, Fletcher

Henderson, Artie Shaw, Bob Crosby, and others were packing them in in theaters and ballrooms all across the country. Such famous sidemen as Charlie Barnet, Harry James, Gene Krupa, Teddy Wilson, Charlie Spevac, Lionel Hampton, and Bob Haggart were celebrities in their own right. Vocal groups and soloists traveling with the big bands skyrocketed to fame and fortune. The legendary Frank Sinatra got his start as a vocalist with the Harry James and Tommy Dorsey Orchestras. Others who gained popularity as vocal soloists included June Christy, Anita O'Day, Joe Stafford, Doris Day, and Mel Torme. Tex Benke, who played tenor saxophone with the Glen Miller band, became almost as well known as a vocalist as Miller's featured tenor saxophonist. Every kid in the country who played any kind of musical instrument dreamed of one day playing with the big bands and was eagerly waiting his or her big chance. I was no exception and I thought I was on my way.

Stan Thal's orchestra consisted of Thal on trumpet and drums, Arlton Hatch and Tommy Wren, two of my classmates and close friends, on reeds, Thal's wife on piano, Rubin Hartman on base, and me on trombone. There were several social clubs in the Kerrville area—the Lancers, the German Club, and others—that we played for regularly. We also played for dances at the Bluebonnet Hotel and for other organizations. It was a new experience for me and, although we were not paid well, I found it exciting. I always felt that Thal took advantage of his young sidemen (Arlton, Tommy, and me) but we were so proud to be in the music business we didn't think much about it.

When I was first asked to play in the band, I was not sure what my parents' reaction would be. Being staunch Southern Baptists, they discouraged dancing, drinking, smoking and all of those kinds of "worldly pleasures." As I mentioned earlier, my parents had always been very protective of me, especially concerning what they considered immoral influences. I was surprised by their reaction when I told them of the opportunity. My mother said: "C. C., you know how we feel about such things, but it is up to you. You decide for yourself." I had not expected that kind of response. I took the job.

The church was always very important to our family. We always went to Sunday school and church. After I started playing in the band, I didn't get to bed before two or three o'clock Sunday morning because we often played for dances on Saturday nights. Even so, I remember getting up Sunday mornings and going to Sunday school and church and singing in the choir.

At the end of my junior year, Stan Thal moved away from Kerrville. Arlton and I took over the dance band. We added Manley Cooper to the reed section and Roger Thorson took over on drums. They were both a year behind Arlton and me in school. Our big problems were piano and trumpet. We finally recruited one of the local piano teachers, Mrs. Jones. She was a widow and had a son about our age. She was a good sport and unquestionably a much better musician than any of the rest of us. She wasn't used to playing our kind of music, though, and we had to loosen her up a bit. Looking back, I don't know how she put up with us. But she seemed to enjoy us and tried to have a steadying influence.

The trumpet replacement was more difficult. In fact, I think we played a couple of jobs without a trumpet, with me taking the brass lead on trombone. There was no one in high school who played good trumpet and no one else in town who was interested in joining us.

Finally, purely by accident, we heard of an older fellow who lived out in the sticks who played trumpet. We finally located him—I can't even remember his name now—and he jumped at the chance to play with us. He was probably in his late 20s at the time, and he was in love with the trumpet. He was a bachelor and lived with his parents in the country. He rode a motorcycle and would come breezing into town, his trumpet in a bag slung over his shoulder. He was somewhat of a character, but a nice guy. He played good trumpet by ear and was trying to learn to read music. He was one of the best at improvisation, but he wasn't very good when playing in ensemble. We featured him solo a lot and got by very well with him. He could play almost anything after he heard it once.

I lived music night and day. I got every record that had a great trombone man on it that I could get my hands on. I played each record over and over listening to such trombone greats as George Brunis, J.C. Higginbotham, Benny Morton, Tommy Dorsey, and of course my idol, Jack Teagarden. I would sometimes play along with them and often try to copy their hot licks (probably not too successfully) in our band.

Arlton and I read *Down Beat* and *Metronome* magazines religiously, keeping up with the latest changes in personnel within the bands, and what and who were leading on the charts. We would listen to Benny Goodman every night on his network broadcast, "Let's Dance." Since he came on between eleven o'clock and midnight, we had to keep the radio turned down so as not to awaken my parents.

Arlton and I bought plywood and made fancy music stands. We called the band the "Kerrville Notes." We had the name painted on the new stands with some quarter and eighth notes scattered around. They looked very classy. When we got the band organized, we had three reeds (Arlton, lead alto sax, Manley on tenor, and Tommy on alto), trumpet and trombone, and drums and piano. Mr. Hartman dropped out when Thal left and we didn't replace him. We continued to play the clubs and added jobs at the camps up the river in the summer. We were pretty good and developed a good following which gave us as many bookings as we could handle. We continued to play through the summer after I graduated from high school, but the band disbanded following that. Three of us graduated together, Arlton, Tommy, and I, which left the group without much leadership.

In my high school years I was quite popular. I dated some of the prettiest girls in school. It was said that the prettiest girl in a room would be C. C.'s date. I don't know why I had such good luck with the girls, but I enjoyed it. While my buddies played the field, I usually dated one girl at a time. There were Claire Stehling, Beatrice LeBlanc, and Dorothy Bynum, whom I remember. But my real first love was Mary Sue Ross.

Mary Sue was a petite blond who was very popular and a very good student. I still remember the time I first asked her for a date. It was in the summer following my junior year in high school. We met in front of the post office, I was coming out and she was going in. On the spur of the moment, I asked her for a date; to my surprise she accepted. She was a grade behind me in school, and although I knew who she was, I had not had any association with her before. That was the start of a romance that lasted the rest of my high school days. We went "steady" for over a year. In my senior year, we were elected Tivy High School Sweethearts by the student body and had our pictures featured in the yearbook.

In the spring of 1938, I graduated from Tivy High School. I never saw a scholastic ranking of my class, but I am sure I would have been near the bottom. I think the only reason they graduated me was that they needed my seat the next year. The school superintendent, Dr. Moore, was a friend of my parents, he and his family being active members of the same church our family attended. During my senior year, Dr. Moore said to my father: "Curtis, you don't have any plans for C.C. to go to college, do you? If you do, I can tell you it would be a waste of time and money." Based on my performance up to that time, I must agree with his assessment.

The only automobile wreck I have ever had occurred the day of my graduation. That afternoon I drove to the cleaning shop to pick up my graduation gown for the exercises that evening. On my way back home, I collided with another car at the intersection of Jefferson and Washington Streets. The driver of the other car was a Mexican man with his wife and several children. Fortunately, no one was injured, but both cars were damaged. My father's car, which I was driving, had a crumpled front fender, but it was still drivable. Although the driver of the other car was at fault, the police were not called and no one was ticketed. Things were simpler in those days than they are now.

In May, 1938, I received my high school diploma. I had no idea what lay ahead for me and probably gave it little thought. I went through the normal feelings of sadness and relief. A new era in my life was beginning; although I didn't recognize it at the time, I was ill-equipped for it. But in my youthful fearlessness, I plunged ahead not knowing what awaited me "out there."

IV

Some Growing Up

In the fall of 1938, Dr. Moore's advice to my father notwithstanding, I entered Howard Payne College, Brownwood, Texas, as a freshman. The major reason for selecting Howard Payne was Dr. Z.T. Huff, a family friend and former business partner of my father's in Plainview, who was then dean at Howard Payne. He had formerly been dean of Wayland College in Plainview.

Howard Payne was a four-year liberal arts Baptist college. Two high school classmates, Frank Fisher and Harold Hatch, also enrolled at Howard Payne that year. Frank had been a close friend throughout my years in Kerrville. He went to Howard Payne on a football scholarship, and during his four years there made quite a name for himself as a quarterback. He had a high school coaching career after college.

Harold was a cousin of my close friend Arlton Hatch. Like Arlton's, Harold's family lived on a ranch, some distance from Kerrville, so he stayed in Kerrville to go to high school. He and I had been good friends during high school, but we were not as close as Arlton and I. He was not the good student that Arlton was. He went to Howard Payne only because I did; we were roommates our first semester. Arlton went to Texas University in Austin to study engineering.

I went to Howard Payne on a music scholarship to play in the college band. Before being awarded the scholarship, I had to audition for the director. The day of the audition, Arlton went with me to Brownwood to look over the college. During my audition, he was sitting just outside the door to the practice room where he could hear me. The director had me play several marches and concert pieces. Afterwards Arlton said I sounded awful. The problem was that I was not used to playing music of that type, having played practically nothing but jazz and swing for the prior two years. He said I really made the marches jump. We had a big laugh over it. I got the scholarship anyway and easily adjusted to the strict cadence of the band music. I was soon playing first chair trombone.

At Howard Payne I didn't apply myself to my studies any better than I had in high school. I flunked out at the end of the semester and moved back home. Dr. Moore had been correct.

At the start of the spring semester, I enrolled in Schreiner Institute, which was located in Kerrville. I could live at home and reduce the cost. Schreiner Institute was a military school that included high school and two years of college. I didn't do any better at Schreiner than I had at Howard Payne. In fact, being a military school, the rules were more strict, and I soon found myself on the drill field, much of my free time, walking off demerits. Before the end of the semester I quit. Once again Dr. Moore was correct.

During the time I was at Schreiner Institute, my father closed his store. I suppose the competition was too great; by that time there were two larger grocery stores in the same block as the Dixie Market.

My father acquired a large truck and he and I started hauling oranges and grapefruit from the Rio Grande Valley to northern Texas, primarily the Wichita Falls and Amarillo areas. The distance to Amarillo was about 800 miles and to Wichita Falls somewhat less. After loading in the Valley we would leave in the evening, and taking turns at the wheel we would drive straight through to our destination. Those were grueling trips, taking up to 20 hours. There were no superhighways, although the highways were well-maintained hard surface roads.

During those trips, my father and I got to know each other and had a closer relationship than we had ever had before. He had a good sense of humor and was never at a loss for words. It was during those trips that I learned a lot about my father and the family, much of which is reflected in this writing.

After we arrived at our destination, sometimes we would be there for several days, depending on how long it took to sell our load. Some nights we slept in the truck and some nights in a motel. We got along well together and enjoyed each other's company. Time permitting, we would take in a show or take advantage of other entertainment opportunities. I remember us standing in line in Wichita Falls, a considerable length of time, to see *Gone With the Wind* when it first came out. Looking back I see those as very good times, contributing a great deal to my maturing.

My father was a very intelligent and well-read man. Although his formal education was limited, he was very astute and knowledgeable in many areas. I know he attended high school in Temple, Oklahoma, because he told me about playing football at Temple High School. I am not certain that he graduated. He attended a business college in Oklahoma City and was very good at business mathematics. Sometime in his early years he aspired to be a lawyer. In those days many would-be lawyers studied under a practicing attorney rather than attending law school. They called this "reading the law," and when sufficiently knowledgeable, they took the bar examination. My father read the law in a lawyer's office in Oklahoma but never took the bar examination.

My father was a life-long Republican. He was the political black sheep in his family; all the rest of the family was Democrats. He would be classified as a Conservative Republican today. He abhorred anything that hinted at socialism, he was uncompromisingly committed to the free enterprise system, and he believed that "every tub must sit on its own bottom." According to him, that meant that if you wanted something done you had to do it for yourself without depending on the government, society, your family, or friends. He would have loved President Ronald Reagan.

He thought that Franklin D. Roosevelt was the Antichrist. I think that during Roosevelt's first years in office my father was convinced that the country would not survive as a free and independent nation beyond his first term. All of the drastic measures included in Roosevelt's New Deal programs, in my father's opinion, would eventually enslave the nation. I remember his vehemently condemning the new Social Security system—pure socialism he said. The irony is that in his later years he benefited from Social Security payments. My father's political philosophy must have had an impact on me as I have always voted Republican. I am not the conservative that he was, though. I consider myself more middle-of-the-road in politics.

In religion my father was just as conservative. He was raised a Southern Baptist and lived in the "Bible Belt" all of his life. He taught Sunday school classes and sang in the church choir. He played piano and loved to sing. Our family used to sing as a quartet, mainly for our own enjoyment: Hazel singing soprano, Mother alto, Daddy tenor, and I bass. (I was not really a bass so I missed many of the very low notes.)

I was the only one in the family who did not play the piano. When I was young I started piano lessons, but after awhile I wanted to quit and my parents let me. Hazel, on the other hand, took lessons, and our parents made her stay with it. I wished in later years that my parents had made me stay with it too.

My father was very opinioned and had no tolerance for anything off-color or immoral. Anyone who breached his standards of conduct was soundly condemned in no uncertain terms. He would not hesitate to call their transgressions to their attention and also express his disapproval of such acts to anyone else. I have heard him take other men to task for using what he considered vulgar language in the presence of women. Even a "damn" or "hell" met with his condemnation. I never in my life heard him use any vulgarity or curse words of any kind.

My father was intelligent, informed, responsible, law-abiding, and of high moral standards. He had good business sense and made friends easily. With all of his good qualities, I have never understood why he was not able to recover, financially, from the depression.

In the summer of 1939, after the citrus season was over, we hauled watermelons and other in-season fruits and vegetables. In the fall we even hauled hay from South Texas to North Texas where it was in demand for winter feeding.

In late 1939 or early 1940, we moved to Oklahoma. We moved into the little red house on my Aunt Birdie's farm, which was located about midway between Walters and Temple. We were two miles from the old home place where my father was raised. My grandfather had died in 1936, but my grandmother still lived there with Aunt Birdie and her two daughters. Also, my father's Uncle Kansas, who was getting up in years, still lived there. Aunt Zilla, my father's oldest sister, and her husband, Charlie Thompson, lived on her farm that was near the farm we lived on. Her son, Harlin, and his wife, Nova, also lived on Aunt Zilla's farm but in a separate house. So, we were in the midst of family—my grandmother, aunts, uncles, and cousins.

My father and I helped with the farming on my grandmother's farm, as well as Aunt Birdie's and Aunt Zilla's. We also hired out to other farmers in the area. I plowed, cultivated crops, helped in the harvests, sheared sheep, and picked cotton. Uncle Charlie still operated an old-style thrashing machine; all of the other farmers had gone to new, less labor-intensive combines for harvesting their wheat and oats. Uncle Charlie had two thrashing machines, but he operated only one while scavenging parts from the other to keep one running. He still thrashed grain for several of the farmers who had been his customers for years.

I worked for Uncle Charlie during the harvest time, usually pitching bundles. This involved gathering the wheat or oat bundles from the field, stacking them on the bundle wagon using a long-handled pitchfork, and hauling them to the thrashing machine. At the thrashing machine the bundles were fed into the machine, the grain came out into a truck, and the straw was blown into a straw stack. Harvest time was in the hottest part of the summer, and the straw and chaff sticking to your sweat-drenched body was most uncomfortable.

Uncle Charlie always operated short-handed using only two bundle wagons, one of which I ran. My cousin Harlin ran the thrashing machine, and Uncle Charlie hauled the grain to the storage barn or to town. With only two bundle wagons, we could not keep up with the thrasher. Consequently, much of the time the thrashing machine was shut down waiting for bundles. Also, much time was lost due to mechanical breakdowns. Harlin was also the mechanic. With used parts from the other old machine, and lots of bailing wire, he kept us going. This was not a very efficient operation. It was easy to understand why other farmers had gone to combines.

The big treat during thrashing time was the meals. It was customary for the farmer for whom you were thrashing to provide the noon meal. It seemed like every farmer's wife tried to outdo her neighbor. Those were truly feasts. It was always hard to get back in the swing of things after a meal. It was good that we got lots of exercise; otherwise the crew would have gained many pounds during harvest time.

Uncle Charlie was one of my favorite characters. He was Aunt Zilla's second husband, whom she married after the death of her first husband. Her only child, Harlin, was from her first marriage. Uncle Charlie had not been married before. The Thompson family had been neighbors of the Harlins in the Pioneer Community for many years.

In earlier years, Uncle Charlie sold Raleigh products throughout the community. In those days, nearly every community had its Raleigh man who sold household products from his car or truck. The Raleigh line included all kinds of spices, condiments, and household remedies such as liniments and cough syrup. I remember how I enjoyed the Raleigh mustard when I visited as a young boy. Uncle Charlie was not the most energetic person in the world. I wouldn't say he was lazy; he was just careful not to exert himself. He wore extremely thick eyeglasses that greatly magnified his eyes. Because of his poor vision, he tended to walk very gingerly with a Chaplin-like shuffle. His appearance and mannerisms reminded one of a cartoon character.

As mentioned before, his job on the thrashing crew was hauling the grain to the barn. Even when running uninterrupted, it took considerable time to fill his truck. Under normal operation we had a lot of downtime so Uncle Charlie spent most of his time waiting for a load of grain. During these times he would always find a nice shady place to nap while he waited.

When Uncle Charlie got involved in anything strenuous—which was seldom—his standard comment was, "That really makes your colt kick." For the longest time I didn't know what this expression meant. One day I asked him about it. He explained that when you work a mare that is in foal, very hard, you can see the unborn colt kicking the mare's side. Thus the origin of the expression.

In the fall of 1940, I got a job in the shoe department of Mooney's Department Store in Temple. Temple was a very small town with a population of only a few hundred, and Mooney's was the primary business establishment. The Mooney brothers had been in business there for many years and had built a thriving business. I spent several months selling shoes.

One summer, while living on Aunt Birdie's farm, we were visited by Hazel and her two children, Hazel Marie and Curtis Henry. They were about four and six years old, respectively. They had always lived in town, so they had lots of fun being on the farm, seeing the cows, chickens, and pigs. Shortly after they arrived, one of the children came down with the mumps. In the following days, there was a new case in the family almost daily. Before it ended we all had the mumps except Hazel, who had already had them, and my mother. It was very difficult for my father and me. My father was the last one to have them and we thought we were going to lose him.

Early in 1941 my father and I got jobs as carpenters at Fort Sill, Lawton, Oklahoma, which was located about 25 miles from where we lived. As the country came nearer to war, there were big building projects at most military installations, including Fort Sill. Craftsmen of all kinds, carpenters, plumbers, painters, etc, were in demand. Almost anyone who had a saw and hammer could become a carpenter. All one had to do was join the union and they could be hired.

My father had no trouble passing the tests for journeyman carpenter. I took the tests and was classified a second-year apprentice. We became card-carrying members of the United Brotherhood of Carpenters and Joiners of America and went to work.

The pay was good and you could work almost as many hours as you wanted to. I had a lot to learn but had always been mechanically inclined and good with my hands. I was soon doing the work of a journeyman, though without the pay. I helped build hundreds of "six-man huts" as well as other types of buildings. The six-man huts were 16-foot square structures that accommodated six men. They were constructed of plywood with a pyramidal roof. They had no interior walls or accessories; the only furnishings were the six cots the men slept on and their six footlockers. These huts were used at all military bases to house the thousands of troops that were being trained for the war.

Sunday morning, December 7, 1941, I went to church at the Pioneer School where I led the singing. I stayed around home in the afternoon and early evening decided to go into town. As I drove down Main Street of Walters it was alive with people, which was unusual for Sunday night. I parked and got out of the car and asked the first person I met, an elderly farmer in overalls, "What's going on?" "Haven't you heard?" He replied. "The Japanese have bombed the 'Honoluluian' Islands." This was my first knowledge of the Pearl Harbor attack that plunged our nation into World War II and that drastically altered my life. How it changed my life! At that time I could not have predicted all of the changes.

In the days following the Pearl Harbor attack, recruiting centers throughout the country were inundated with volunteers, able-bodied men (some not so able-bodied) showing their patriotism. On December 10, my friends Bill Ogletree and Alvin Painter (both lived in Walters) and I hitched-hiked to Oklahoma City to enlist in the Army Air Corps. (The U.S. Air Force, as we have today, was not created as a separate service until after the war.)

Bill Ogletree had a girlfriend, Ann Capps from Comanche, Oklahoma, who was living in Oklahoma City attending Draughon's Business College. That evening Bill and I went to her downtown apartment and met her and Darla Alene Apple, who also attended Draughon's and shared the apartment. I don't remember Alvin's going; he must have found something else to do. Alene (in those days she went by her middle name) was also from Comanche and she and Ann had been close friends since before grade school. Bill and Ann dated while Ann was still in Comanche, Comanche being only about 20 miles from Walters. Alene and I got along very well; little did I know what would come from this meeting.

During that visit to Oklahoma City I acquired a nickname, which even today has stuck with those who knew me then. I don't recall exactly how it came about, but someone, in jest, called me "Curley" because my hair, in contrast, was very straight. I seldom see friends of that era, but if I do, they still call me Curley.

Early the next morning, Bill, Alvin, and I went to the Army Recruiting Center to enlist in the Air Corps for pilot training. Bill knew he would not be accepted because he had previously tried to enlist and had been rejected for physical reasons. The results of a football injury in high school, which left nerve damage, kept him out. He tried again anyway with the same negative results.

First, we were given a battery of written tests to determine our aptitude and knowledge in a number of areas and our I.Q. This consumed most of the morning. I did very well on all of these tests. Next was the physical examination. Again I had no problem; however I did fail to tell the doctors about my history of asthma.

The very last part of the physical examination was the eyes. I knew I was home free because I had never had any eye problems. I read the eye chart; the doctor looked into my eyes with the little light beam, and then had me read the little book used to determine color blindness. As the doctor turned the pages I had no trouble calling out letters and figures. Closing the book on the last page, he asked, "How many of those do you think you got right?" "All of them," I confidently replied. "You got seven right." I could not believe it. I don't know exactly how many pages there were in the book but there must have been 25 or 30. He then went back through it and asked me what I saw in the dots on the pages. He would correct me and trace, with his finger, the correct figure. I hadn't known before that I was colorblind. I have never had any problem identifying the basic colors, but I do have some trouble with shades and pastels. This condition kept me out of pilot training in World War II.

Alvin successfully passed all of the tests and went through pilot training and was sent to England as a B-17 pilot. He was shot up pretty badly in missions over Germany but survived the war. I think he stayed in the service until retirement, but I am not positive. As for Bill and me, we returned to Walters. I was disappointed but was not ready to enlist in any of the other services, so I resumed my carpentry job at Fort Sill.

I had heard of young men from the U.S.A. going to Canada and enlisting in the Royal Canadian Air Force (RCAF). This was not in any way like our young men going to Canada during the Vietnam War to avoid the draft. This was perfectly legal and rather than avoiding combat, exposed them to combat even before we entered the war. It was also known that Canada's requirements were not as rigorous as ours, and the kind of color blindness I had would not keep me out. Shortly after returning from Oklahoma City, I wrote to Canada to volunteer for the RCAF. I received a nice letter of reply thanking me, but informing me that since the entrance of our country into the war, they were no longer taking enlistees from the U.S.A.

Our enlistees in the RCAF presented an interesting dilemma for our Army Air Corps after we entered the war. Those RCAF flyers were required to change over to our Air Corps, but most of them were enlisted men. All pilots in our Air Corps were commissioned officers. Thus, early in the war we had the "Flying Sergeants." Not many people today are aware that we had enlisted pilots then. Later, the rank of Flight Officer was created which corresponded to Warrant Officer. The Flying Sergeants became Flight Officers and restored respectability to the service.

Alene and I started dating regularly. On weekends Bill and I would go to Oklahoma City to see Alene and Ann, usually hitch-hiking. Unlike today, in those days it was easy to get rides. Some weekends Alene would come home, and I would see her there. As the weeks passed we began to get serious.

Everything was geared to the war effort. Defense plants turning out ammunition, airplanes, and all types of military vehicles and armament were operating around the clock. Women were flocking to the plants in great numbers, doing jobs that had been done only by men before. Rationing of all sorts of consumer items was imposed. The draft was in high gear and enlistments were booming. Military construction escalated and I continued to do my part as a carpenter at Fort Sill.

V

"You're in the Army Now"

In the late summer of 1942, I decided it was time for me to enlist. I quit my job and off I went to Oklahoma City to join the Army. Of course I was eligible for the draft, but I wasn't subject to call very soon. I had no desire for the Navy; I couldn't even swim. The Army was my choice.

I will never forget the day I left home to go to Oklahoma City to enlist. I told a tearful mother good-by in the house. Daddy was in the barn, so I walked down there as I was leaving to tell him good-by. If I had ever had any doubt about his loving me, it would have been dispelled during that good-by.

Daddy had not been in World War I. He was of draft age, but was rejected for physical reasons. In his youth he was thrown from a horse and hit his head on a rock, which gave him a concussion. The rest of his life he had a fairly large indention in the top of his skull, although it never caused him any problem. When he was called up to take his physical examination, the examining physician felt the indentation in his head. After my father explained its origin, he was rejected. Such minor conditions were not sufficient for rejection during World War II. But back to that summer morning in 1942.

Daddy and I engaged in trivial conversation, both of us not sure what to say and wanting to maintain our manliness. My father was not an emotional person and never showed any outward signs of affection. That morning was probably the closest I ever saw him come to letting go of his feelings. As I left I will never forget what he said: "I wish there was a way I could go in your place." I think he really meant it. With that I hit the road for Oklahoma City.

On August 21, 1942, I was sworn into the U.S. Army in Oklahoma City and given the Army Serial Number (ASN) of 18130949—no one ever forgets their ASN. Our group was loaded on a train in Oklahoma City, and we arrived at the processing center at Fort Sill about dusk. The next morning was the beginning of hours upon hours of standing in lines, an activity that would occupy much of our time for the next several days. We received our shots, were issued our clothing, and attended lectures and orientation films, interspersed between periods of standing in line. Because of my experience I was classified a carpenter, which didn't sit very well with me. I hadn't joined the Army to drive nails.

After three or four days at Fort Sill, we were divided into groups to be sent to our basic training stations. The group I was in went by train to Lackland Field in San Antonio, Texas. Nothing much happened for several days. Most of the time we were free to do as we pleased but were not allowed to leave the base. As the days passed, rumors spread that we had been sent there by mistake, and they didn't know what to do with us. After a couple of weeks of this, we were again loaded onto a train, which headed east to our destination, Camp Gordon, Georgia. At last I had arrived at the site where I would endure my basic training.

We were immediately put to work: up before daybreak every morning, close order drill, target practice, long marches, and simulated combat. These and other training activities filled our days. Falling into bed late at night was welcomed relief for my poor aching body, but it seemed that no sooner had I fallen asleep than it was "rise and shine" time and time to do it all again. Everyday was the same, but finally I was declared a soldier and it was over—I thought.

When I enlisted I had not stated any preference for assignment, so I had no idea where I was going. Once again I was on a train—destination Dale Mabry Field, Tallahassee, Florida. Dale Mabry was a fighter base having mostly P-38, P-39, and P-47 aircraft. Arriving at Dale Mabry Field I found that I was in the Ordnance Branch of the Army attached to the Air Corps. Ordnance? I had on idea what it was.

In the days ahead I began to believe that Ordnance had to do with the mess hall. I was on K.P. (kitchen police) almost full-time. Other than that duty I didn't do much. Occasionally we would go out on some kind of exercises, but they were not very exciting. The unit I was in was commanded by a tough old major. Major Pfeiffer was a career enlisted man before the war and, like many enlisted men, was given a temporary promotion due to the shortage of officers. His permanent rank was master sergeant, we were told.

One night, not very long after arriving at Dale Mabry Field, I was awakened and told that my sister was at the main gate. This was a complete surprise to me. I hurriedly dressed and ran to the gate and just outside in their car were Hazel, Henry, and their two children Curtis Henry and Hazel Marie. They were moving from Kerrville to Portsmouth, Virginia. Henry was a sheet metal worker and had taken a job in the shipyard in the Portsmouth/Norfolk area. We visited for a while, and then they continued on their way to Virginia. I would not see them again until after the war.

That fall I was one of three from Dale Mabry Field selected to attend Aircraft Armament School in East Lansing, Michigan. We stayed in a dormitory on the campus of Michigan State University and attended classes at the Oldsmobile plant. The Oldsmobile plant had been converted to defense work including the manufacture of 50-caliber machine guns and 20-millimeter and 37-millimeter aircraft cannons.

Those six weeks were good duty. The training was very intense, but in the evenings and on weekends we had a lot of freedom. East Lansing was not very exciting, but the town welcomed the soldiers, and everyone was very friendly. During the week curfew for us was about 10 p.m., which, after classes and dinner, didn't leave much time to relax and unwind in town. Consequently, many of us would miss curfew regularly. The punishment was not severe though. It consisted of staying after dinner and helping clear the mess hall. Civilians ran the mess and, with the number of GIs assigned to the duty, it didn't take long to do the job. Those of us on K.P. were in town almost as soon as those who were not.

Our class ended right before Christmas. The final examination consisted of disassembling and reassembling a machine gun and the two aircraft cannons, blindfolded. It was a timed test, and although I don't remember my time, I did very well. It is amazing how easy this was after learning every part of the weapons, intimately, during the class. The secret was laying out the parts in an orderly fashion so you knew exactly where they were and not dropping any.

We were all granted leave until after Christmas. I remember having Christmas dinner with a nice family in East Lansing. Many families showed their patriotism during the war by "adopting" the GIs and having them in their homes. The song *White Christmas*, sung by Bing Crosby, was just out and very popular at that time. It is still heard at Christmas, and every time I hear it I am reminded of my Christmas in East Lansing, Michigan.

Not very long after returning to Dale Mabry Field, I was transferred to a small sub-base of Dale Mabry located near Thomasville, Georgia. The Thomasville Air Field was just being built and the ordnance section consisted of another GI from Dale Mabry by the name of Ronigen (I don't recall his first name) and me. He was a tall, wiry, blond-headed cowboy from Montana. He looked like he could have been straight out of a western movie, and we became very good friends. Corporal Ronigen was in charge; I was Private First

Class at the time. We set up business in a small wooden shack.

The base was still under construction when we moved in and, therefore, there were no aircraft to service. We began to receive shipments of ammunition and small arms—pistols, revolvers, shotguns, and machine guns. The small building we occupied was far from adequate; it was filled very soon. Worse, it was not a secure place for the storage of weapons and ammunition. This was proved in a dramatic way one morning when we arrived to find that the building had been broken into. We discovered that a number of Thompson sub-machine guns had been taken.

During the next few days, Ronigen and I spent hours with military authorities and FBI agents answering questions and giving information. To my knowledge, the weapons were never recovered, but the case was made that we were not equipped to handle any more shipments.

When construction was completed aircraft began to arrive. We had the same aircraft as Dale Mabry Field, P-38s, P-39s, and P-47s. Later some B-25s were added. A new ordnance area was built on the edge of the field, which included a warehouse and office building and bomb storage bunkers, all inside a high-security fence. As we moved into our new facility, our staff grew. Lieutenant Clifford Tilton was assigned as Ordnance Officer and several enlisted men were added, including Tech Sergeant Christensen, Sergeant George Shaw, and Private Boston. While Ronigen and I had been the entire complement, we enjoyed a leisurely life. After we moved into our new area, and the base reached full strength, the work picked up.

The ordnance group was responsible for the procurement, storage, and issuing of ammunition and bombs only. We had no responsibility for servicing the weapons; the squadrons handled that. We handled ammunition for the aircraft machine guns and cannons and also small arms. The bombs we stored were mostly 100-pound practice bombs but we also had bombs as large as 1,000 pounds. We hauled the ammunition and bombs from Dale Mabry Field by truck and bomb trailer, a distance of about 50 miles.

Early in my assignment at Thomasville, I was sent to bomb disposal school. I became an "expert" at disarming and removing damaged or malfunctioning bombs. Fortunately, I was seldom called on to demonstrate my expertise. Occasionally a plane would return from a practice-bombing mission over the Gulf of Mexico with a bomb, which had not released properly, that had to be removed.

The Thomasville Air Field, being small, did not have an authorized band. I heard of some guys who were trying to organize a dance band, and I looked them up. I met Louis Dellcini, the leader, and told him I would like to be included. He didn't have a trombone player and was glad to have me. We were soon in business with the standard three reeds, three brasses, and three rhythms. Louis was a very fine trumpet man who had played with Lou Prima before being drafted. Others had had good professional experience prior to their induction into the army.

A big surprise was discovering that Cleve Wheelis, whom I had known in Kerrville, was playing saxophone and clarinet. Cleve was a year or two behind me in high school but I knew him well. There were two other Texans I remember: another reed man named Burnette from West Texas and the guitar player, Larry Wing, from Corpus Christi. He played real fine guitar and had done lots of good work in civilian days. Our piano player, whose last name was Thomas; looked and acted more like a farm hand than a musician. But when he sat down at the piano, you knew he was something special. He was probably the best technical musician we had. Our drummer's name was Swartz who, like most drummers, was the group's clown-in-residence. Our band went by the name The Militairs.

Our base had an officer's club, but drinking and card playing were the principal activities. We were soon booked to play a dance there, which led to our being engaged there regularly. A major, who practically lived at the club, was Base Transportation Officer. He took a liking to us and volunteered that we could have any vehicles we needed any time. In a short time, we were playing jobs in southern Georgia and northern Florida for civilian as well as military events. We even played at the Dale Mabry Officers Club, although they had a base band and their own dance band. We stayed together for over a year and did lots of jobs. The money I made in the band exceeded my meager Army pay.

While I was in the Army, my parents moved to Fort Worth, Texas; Daddy was working in the Consolidated Aircraft factory helping build the B-24 bomber. He was in the procurement end of the operation and took great pride in his job. My mother had gone to work at Montgomery Ward, which had a very large retail and mail order operation in Fort Worth. When the family heard that she had gone to work, we could hardly believe it; she had never worked outside the home. Furthermore, she was fairly shy and did not appear to be suited for a retail sales clerk. It was hard to get help during the war years, and she wanted to do her part.

During the war, blood drives were held frequently to supply the much needed blood for our battlefield casualties. Mother, again wanting to do her part for the war effort, presented herself at the Red Cross Center to give blood. The nurse had difficulty getting the needle into a vein, making numerous attempts; it seemed that her veins were very small. Finally, the nurse gave up and thanked my mother for her valiant try. My father said that when she came home, both of her arms were black and blue from her wrists to her elbows, a most pitiful sight. Mother, being the silent sufferer she was, only regretted that she was unable to help those in need.

Alene and I had maintained a steady flow of letters, and were making plans to get married when I could get a furlough. With the uncertain future and the romance of the boys marching off to war, many young people were swept into marriage. Early in June 1943, I got my first furlough and returned to Oklahoma to tie the knot.

After I had enlisted in the Army, Alene graduated from business college and was employed in Oklahoma City. Also, her parents had moved to Duncan, Oklahoma, which was only about 10 miles north of Comanche. I met Alene in Duncan, and on Saturday evening, June 5, 1943, we were married in the First Methodist Church at Duncan by the pastor, Dr. Flynn. Alene had been raised a Methodist.

We had a small wedding attended by only family and a small number of friends. My parents came from Fort Worth, the only members of my family attending. Ann and Bill Ogletree (they had married a few months earlier), who had been responsible for our meeting, were our attendants. There was nothing fancy about the wedding; I wore my khaki GI-issue uniform of a Private First Class.

That night, in a car borrowed from some of the family, we started looking for a room for the night. We tried all the hotels and motels in Duncan; they were all full. Duncan was only about 20 miles from Fort Sill, and on the weekends the soldiers filled up every available bed. Finally, in desperation, Alene called one of her cousins and explained our predicament to him and his wife. We were invited to their home where we spent our wedding night.

A day or two after the wedding, we went to Fort Worth and spent the remainder of my furlough with my parents. Housing was in short supply due to the war, so my parents had rented a very small apartment in a private home. Alene and I were given their bedroom, and they doubled up some place in the house.

At the end of my furlough, I returned to Thomasville alone. We were so poor that we didn't have enough money for Alene to accompany me. After two or three months, we had saved enough so Alene could join me. In preparation for her arrival, I rented a place in town. What a disaster! It was in an old Victorian home that had been chopped up to create as many rental units as possible. Our bedroom was on the second floor, and our combination kitchen and eating area was crammed in what formerly was a back porch on the first floor. We shared the bath on the second floor, and also shared the refrigerator downstairs. This was far from ideal for a young bride's first home. It wasn't very long before a downstairs unit became available and we moved into it. This "apartment" was not much of an improvement, but at least it was all on the same floor.

Sergeant Christensen, called Chris, lived in the same house. He was single, a career soldier, much older than we, and we became very good friends. He had a car and, somehow, always had plenty of gasoline, in spite of rationing. He took us everywhere, and I rode back and forth to the base with him.

We also became very good friends with Lt. Tilton and his wife. They had not been married much longer than we had and also lived in town. Lt. Tilton had been an enlisted man at Dale Mabry Field when he went to Officers Candidate School. He was returned to his old base following his commissioning, which was very unusual. Normally, a newly commissioned officer was not returned to the unit he served in as an enlisted man. Tilton was always an enlisted man at heart. This did not sit very well with his fellow officers. He didn't go to the officers club and didn't socialize with his fellow officers. He and his wife, George Shaw and his wife, Dorothy, and Alene and I were together often. We had dinner together almost weekly and went together to the movies or other places frequently. We often included Chris and Ronigen.

Shortly after Alene joined me, she got a Civil Service job as a secretary at the military hospital in Thomasville. Her pay was very good for the times and together with my pay and what I made playing in the band we did quite well. As a government civilian employee, Alene was eligible to live in the Three Toms Inn. This inn was a very plush resort hotel that had been turned over to the government for wartime housing. She put her name on the waiting list soon after she started to work, and it wasn't long before we moved in.

This was really luxury living; we had a nice large room with private bath on the ground floor. All of the residents took their meals in a common dining room. There were recreational facilities and beautiful grounds to enjoy. This was about as good as a soldier could have in the wartime Army. About the same time we moved in, George and Dorothy Shaw also moved to Three Toms Inn. Dorothy also had a government civilian job. George had a car, so I rode to and from the base with him.

In the latter half of 1944, the generals realized that they were long on air power and short on foot soldiers. After the invasion of Europe on D-Day in June, it looked like we could be in for a long hard-fought land war. Thus, troop priorities were changed. To increase the number of ground troops in the shortest time, airmen and air support troops were reassigned to the infantry.

We began to hear of personnel from Thomasville being transferred to the infantry. Every day Lt. Tilton would go to base headquarters to check the transfer list. Soon, his ordnance people began to show up on the list. Several of us were put on the list and by hook or crook Tilton was able to get us off. Then one day a catastrophe hit us: Lt. Tilton's name showed up on the list. Soon he was gone and so was our protection.

By the end of summer I received orders transferring me to the infantry. I was soon on a train heading for Camp Maxie, located near Paris, Texas. Alene was on her way to Fort Worth, where she lived with my parents until the end of the war. She had no trouble getting a Civil Service job in Fort Worth, and she worked there the rest of the war.

At Camp Maxie, we were given six weeks of very intensive infantry training. My earlier basic training was a tea party compared to this training. The forced marches were killers, we had mock battles with live ammunition, and we slept out much of the time in our pup tents. Before the end of the training it was beginning to get cold, with lots of rain to add to our misery. By the time the training was over, we felt that the battlefields of Europe and the Pacific could not be very bad. Little did we know!

Upon completing the training, I was shipped to Fort Mead, Maryland, which was a processing center for the European Theater. There, we were issued all new clothing and equipment, given all of our shots (again), and were made to sit through orientation lectures and movies. I wasn't there more than a week but did get into Baltimore one weekend before being shipped out.

Next stop was Camp Kilmer, New Jersey, our debarkation point. We were not there more than two or three days before we were loaded onto a Liberty Ship in the Brooklyn Navy Yard and headed across the North Atlantic Ocean. What a ride!

We were in a convoy of several other troop and cargo ships escorted by an assortment of naval ships. The convoy was strung out over several miles. Several times during our eight or nine day trip there were submarine alerts. When they happened, the naval vessels went into their defensive patterns, and we would see the depth charges hurled over their sides, seeking the hidden marauders below. Strict security was observed, including no outside lights or smoking on deck at night.

The north Atlantic is usually very rough in winter, and this was certainly true during our trip. It didn't bode well for those of us who were unaccustomed to the sea. About the second day out, shortly after breakfast, my stomach turned upside down. I lost my breakfast, the previous night's meal and everything else that was in me. This was only the start of nearly complete debilitation for most of the remainder of the trip. Before it was over, there was hardly a man on the ship who was not affected.

I was not aware of the closeness of our quarters on the ship until every hammock above, below, and on either side of me was occupied by a sick GI who had just vomited or was on the verge of vomiting. The stench became almost unbearable; there was no way of escaping it. Even on deck, if one were strong enough to make it topside, the mixture of diesel fumes and vomit was sickening.

The few times I tried to eat a meal, it would stay down only long enough for me to get to the head or the nearest trash can. It seemed as though at every meal we were served green pea soup. For years I could not stand to eat green pea soup and it is still not one of my favorites.

As we neared the European coast, the ocean became calmer, so during the last day or two of the voyage most of us recovered. Before we reached our destination, the convoy broke up with ships going to different ports. The ship I was on was headed for Le Havre, France, a port that had been opened for shipping only a short while. It was still heavily mined and debris and sunken ships were everywhere. It was a very slow and tedious process getting up the estuary to the dock, but in time we docked and, once again, the feel of *terra firma* under foot was welcomed.

We wasted no time moving out; we were soon on a train heading away from the coast. GIs were transported just like livestock. In fact, we traveled in freight cars, which were affectionately known as "40 and Eight" from World War I days. The name came from the designation of their capacity—40 people or eight horses. There were no seats; the floor was covered with straw, and we alternately stood and sat. Some cars had slatted sides, which provided ventilation; others had solid sides so one door had to be left open. As crowded as we were, it was impossible to lie down to rest.

No one knew where we were going. The train had to do a lot of stopping and back tracking due to bridges and tracks being destroyed. After a couple of days, we arrived at Charleville, France, which is near the Belgium border. Outside of Charleville there was a replacement processing center where we were assigned to our units.

In a very short time I was with a group of replacements heading east in a truck. After a day's travel, we reached our destination. We were greeted by a staff sergeant who was probably not as old as I, but obviously had had experience far beyond his years. His clothes were a makeshift of GI issue, which certainly would not have passed inspection in the training camps that I had come from in the states. It was cold and wet and the sergeant had obviously been tramping through the mud. His boots were so mud-covered that the laces were not even distinguishable. As we alighted from the truck, other soldiers in the greeting party eyed us questioningly. As new replacements we stood out in our clean uniforms, which were complete in every detail, in contrast to their muddy and makeshift attire. We did not realize then that only days before, most of them had arrived just as we had, to be greeted with a mixture of skepticism and envy.

I was unique in the group. Most of the replacements were much younger—18 and 19 years old. At 24 years old, I was the "old man." Most of the replacements came over directly from basic training and practically all were privates. As a sergeant I was a rarity among replacements. Of course, I had been in the Army over two years before I was shipped overseas.

We joined our outfit somewhere south of Trier. Replacements were put in platoons and companies where needed and they had no feeling of continuity or history. We were just bodies and the men we joined showed little comradeship. I guess too many replacements had come and gone to feel that there would be any lasting friendships.

Beyond the identity of our platoon and company we had no knowledge of where we fit into the bigger picture. Much later I learned that I was in the 8th Infantry Division.

The most lasting memory I have of those days in early February 1945 is the cold and mud. There had been heavy snow for several weeks, which turned to mud with the troop and vehicular traffic. Snow continued to fall from time to time, adding to our misery. Movement was slow, probably more because of weather-related conditions than because of the Germans.

In the weeks that followed, our division advanced slowly, but by the end of March we were moving very fast, stopping only occasionally for supplies to catch up or for other adjustments. During one of those pauses in action, in mid-April 1945, we were on the edge of a small village. That night many of us slept in a barn that had ample straw for bedding. As we were getting up in the morning, word went around that President Roosevelt had died. He would not see the victory, which was so close at hand. Our new Commander-in-Chief, President Truman, would preside over this historic event. I remember later in the morning we heard that there would be a memorial service in the village church. Many of us attended this service with the village parishioners.

After crossing the Rhine River, the end was in sight. In the west the American and British forces had the Germans in retreat, and the Russians in the east were at the gates of Berlin. The Germans were surrendering in such numbers that it was impossible to keep track of them and provide for their security. My company was one of those assigned to help round up the German prisoners and hold them until they could be dealt with.

Our outfit was ordered to Bad Kreuznach to set up a prisoner of war (POW) camp. We had thousands of POWs with no place to put them. We occupied what had been a German military installation of some kind. We stayed in the three-

and four-story brick barracks, two GIs to a room. It was very nice, comparatively speaking, and much appreciated after being in the mud and rain for several weeks. Our troops occupied all of the available buildings with no housing for our POWs. The installation was on the edge of town and there were acres and acres of vacant land adjacent to it. This became the home for our charges.

Fencing off a large area created an outdoor compound. The fence was probably eight feet high and made of heavy net wire with barbed wire on the top. The prisoners were herded into the compound like cattle. No shelter was provided, but some of the prisoners, in time, did improvise makeshift shelters from crates and boxes that their rations came in. We had a lot of rain and the temperature was still fairly low; the hundreds of POWs were a miserable lot. I was glad to be on the outside looking in.

We pulled guard duty around the clock with guards every few feet all around the outside of the compound. As the misery inside increased, attempted escapes, mostly at night, increased. Before long, shots from the guards were heard throughout the nights. Nearly every morning, dead POWs, who had been shot trying to escape or who had died from exposure, were hauled away.

Shortly after our assignment to Bad Kreuznach I was given the job of Company Clerk of our company. This came about because my service record indicated that I could type. I welcomed the job because it meant I would work indoors and would no longer have to pull guard duty. I enjoyed the job and, as it turned out, it served me well for future duty.

On May 8, 1945, the armistice was effective and war in Europe was over. There had been all kinds of rumors for several days, but when the official word reached us it was as if a very long, bad dream had finally ended. We celebrated night and day. Our supply sergeant was the source of much of our joy; he was of the old school and had his priorities straight. Sometimes we had to wait days for a new pair of socks or underwear, but his supply room was always fully stocked with the best available wines, schnapps, and other kinds of liquor. He was an expert at "moon-light" requisitioning. His foresight provided all of us the means we needed to properly celebrate our victory.

While the war in Europe had ended, the Pacific war still raged. The troop needs in Europe were for occupation forces, while there was need for additional combat troops in the Pacific Theater. An elaborate point system had been devised to determine an individual soldier's eligibility for continued duty or discharge. Points were credited for length of service, length of time overseas, decorations, parenthood, and age. Those with the greatest number of points were assigned to occupation duty or sent home; others were sent to the Pacific Theater.

When the war ended in Europe, I had been in the Army three years, I had been overseas about six months, and had earned two battle stars. When my points were calculated, I had too many to be sent to the Pacific, but not enough to be returned home for discharge. I was destined for occupation duty. I was sent to 7th Army Headquarters in Heidelberg, Germany, where I would spend the remainder of my European tour of duty.

The processing of troops in and out of the European Theater was a big job at that time. Because of my experience as a Company Clerk, I was assigned to the records section, and was soon made a section chief. In that position I had a staff of several enlisted men, and was responsible for updating, maintaining, and preparing the troop's service records for assignment in Europe, deployment to the Pacific, or return home for discharge. At times it was a hectic job and required long hours to meet shipping order requirements.

One day shortly after I had settled into my job at 7th Army Headquarters, I was ordered to report to the colonel. At the appointed time I was ushered into his office; I gave him my snappiest salute. He immediately put me at ease and invited me to sit down. I was wondering what all this cordiality meant. He said that he had looked at my service record and would like to recommend me for a battlefield commission to 2nd Lieutenant, if I agreed. What a shock! I had not done any great heroics or been involved in anything out of the ordinary. I had just done my job as required like thousands of other GIs. After I recovered my voice I told him I would have to think about it and I would let him know, although I knew at that time what my answer would be.

This was the second time I had been encouraged to become a commissioned officer. When I entered the Army, because of my test scores, I had been encouraged to apply for Officers Candidate School. I didn't choose to. The next day I thanked the colonel and turned down his offer. Accepting the commission would have meant a fast trip to the Pacific Theater where, as had been the case in the European Theater, company grade officers—lieutenants and captains—didn't last very long in combat.

On August 6, 1945, the B-29 Superfortress, Enola Gay, dropped the first atomic bomb, ever used by any country, on the Japanese city of Hiroshima. With this act, the world entered the nuclear age. A second bomb was dropped on the city of Nagasaki three days later. These events brought World War II to an end August 14, 1945, when Japan unconditionally surrendered.

The development of the atomic bomb is a fascinating story. Many of the leading scientists of the Western world worked in total secrecy at several locations on what was called the Manhattan Project. Those involved lived and worked in totally contained facilities and under the most stringent security. It is amazing that so much could have been done in those years without public knowledge.

Beginning immediately after the bombs were dropped, and continuing even today, is the controversy over the decision to use the bomb. President Truman defended its use on the basis of bringing the war to a close and avoiding even larger casualties. Opponents believe, among other things, that indications were that Japan was probably on the verge of surrender at the time of the bombings.

From the earliest years of atomic research, scientists saw the enormous potential for peaceful uses of nuclear power. Since the war, the use of nuclear power has expanded to become a major part of the world's energy requirements. Even so, controversy still exists regarding the benefits and dangers of nuclear energy.

Heidelberg was a very interesting old university town. It had escaped the allied bombings that were inflicted on most German cities. The only damage from the war was the destruction of one of the bridges across the Neckar River. The fact that there were adequate usable buildings was the primary reason for choosing Heidelberg for the headquarters of the 7th Army occupation forces.

Sometime later, our Sergeant Major was sent home to be discharged; I was assigned to take his place. I had only three stripes (my rank was T4), but I was made Acting Sergeant Major, which rated six stripes. I acted in that capacity for the remainder of my tour of duty and never received any promotion. Following my discharge, I did receive notice that I had been awarded the Commendation Medal for my service in 7th Army Headquarters.

I stayed busy and the days passed fairly fast. I had time to visit the surrounding area, and although most of the cities and towns were heavily damaged, there were many points of interest. I learned about the history and culture of the Palatinate—the region of which Heidelberg was a major city. The Army set up classes for the troops at Heidelberg University, and I took a photography class. I explored the Heidelberg castle, which overlooked the city from its lofty position atop the mountain on the bank of the Neckar. At Christmas, I was fortunate to obtain leave to visit Switzerland. As I had spent a memorable Christmas two years before in Lansing, Michigan, I spent this one in the snow, high in the Alps, at Davos.

Early spring, 1946, I was finally eligible for rotation to the States to be discharged. After several delays and false starts, I was on a train heading for Antwerp, Belgium. I became acquainted with some soldiers, who had been in Special Services, and who had visited Antwerp before. All they talked about was the good steaks they had had at a restaurant in Antwerp, called Charlie's. As soon as we could, after reaching Antwerp, we all headed to Charlie's. I was not disappointed; the steak was delicious. Of course, after not having any decent fresh beef for so long, anything would have tasted good. In fact, it might have been horsemeat.

In early March our troop ship, a Liberty ship of the same class as the one I came over on, set sail from Antwerp harbor. This time we took the southern route, going down the west coast of Europe, passing near the Azores, and heading across the Atlantic to New York.

Through my acquaintance with the Special Service guys, I got a job as one of the "disk jockeys" on the ship's public address system. Throughout the day we announced the news and played music. My shift was early morning. At about six o'clock I started my program with a wake-up call for the troops. I would open by saying, "Alright, you guys, it's time to rise and puke," followed by some rousing music. This good-morning call didn't go over very well with those who were feeling the sickness of the sea. Fortunately for me, only my few Special Service friends knew my identity. During the day, as I walked around the ship, I would hear threatening remarks about the nut who woke them up in the morning.

A special benefit that came with the public address system job was that I got to bunk in the crew's quarters, rather than in the cramped quarters with the troops. That, plus a comparatively calm sea, made it a pleasant voyage. I didn't have the least bit of seasickness.

One of the thrills of my life was arriving in New York Harbor. From the time we picked up our pilot at Ambrose Light, till we docked, we were escorted by boats, decorated with bunting, streamers, and flags, and playing welcome home music. As we passed the Statue of Liberty, I thought I would choke on the lump in my throat. There was hardly a dry eye among the troops. The feeling of once again being on U.S.A. soil was overwhelming.

There were no delays once we landed. We were put into groups, which would go to the processing center that was nearest to the location of our induction. In my case it was Camp Chaffee, in the northwest corner of Arkansas, since I had enlisted in Oklahoma City. The processing took about two days. We were given physical examinations, issued new uniforms to wear home, told of our rights and opportunities as veterans, and given transportation vouchers to our destinations. Late in the afternoon, of March 20, 1946, I boarded a bus for Oklahoma City, my discharge papers in my hand. I was once again **MR.** Curtis C. Harlin, Jr., private citizen.

I was discharged with the rank of Technician Fourth Class (equivalent to a buck sergeant). As I rode through the eastern Oklahoma countryside that evening, I mused over the past months. I vowed then that if I ever had to go back into the Army, I would start as a general and work down—I hadn't gotten very far doing it the other way.

Although Alene was living in Fort Worth with my parents, she met me in Oklahoma City. We spent the night there and caught the train to Fort Worth the following day. The reunion with Alene and my parents was tearful but happy. It was good to be home.

How fortunate I was. I had spent three and one-half years in the Army, a year of it in the European Theater, with some of that time in combat, and I had returned to my loved ones without a scratch. All of this didn't really hit me until years later. On a trip to Europe in 1990, I visited the American

Cemetery in Luxembourg. There I saw row after row of white grave markers, including that of General George Patton. These were the casualties of battles in the surrounding area that was the area I had been in. Undoubtedly, there were soldiers buried there who had been in the same outfit as I. All I could think was that I could have been one of those buried there. I cried unashamedly.

VI

Becoming an Engineer

In Fort Worth we rented a one-bedroom, upstairs apartment on Saint Louis Avenue, about two blocks from where my parents lived. Our apartment was in a nice brick four-unit building. It was small but adequate for us. I remember that it was not air-conditioned, and in the summer it was very hot. Otherwise it was nice, and we enjoyed being settled for the first time in our married life.

The war, and my years in the Army, caused lasting changes in my outlook on life. Since my days in high school, when I had my introduction to the music world in Stan Thal's dance band, I had thought that I would pursue a career in music. I thought I would be perfectly happy playing in dance halls and nightclubs the rest of my life. With hard work and some luck I might even have my own big band some day, I thought. By the time I was discharged from the Army, this no longer appealed to me. I was a more mature person after the war; I was married and wanted more out of life than that of a transient musician.

The GI Bill of Rights (Serviceman's Readjustment Act of 1944) offered many opportunities for returning servicemen, among which was the means for additional education. I was determined to return to college, but what would I study? From as early as I can remember, I wanted to be a lawyer. I considered studying law, but rejected it because of the length of time it would take to complete a law degree. I didn't want to devote that much time to college before I was ready for a real job.

I considered studying music and looked through several college catalogues. The drawback was that all of them required varying degrees of proficiency in piano. I would have to take piano lessons, and to make any headway I would need a piano at home—which I didn't have. Although I had a great desire for music, this didn't seem very practical.

Having been discharged in March, I had plenty of time to make up my mind before the beginning of the fall semester. Darla (by the end of the war Alene was going by her first name because of the use of her first name in her government jobs during the war years) was working as a secretary for an architectural firm in Fort Worth so our bills were paid. I also had my mustering out money to help out. But after a few days of adjustment, I needed something to do.

We were attending Broadway Baptist Church and were making friends in a young married couples' Sunday school class taught by Gene Smith, a very likable man. Gene was in the insurance business and invited me to join his office. I took him up on his offer and became a representative of the Connecticut Mutual Life Insurance Company. I immediately began studying about the various types of insurance plans and completed a company correspondence course. I found out that there was much more to selling insurance than just writing applications. The thing that was emphasized over and over was that you had to make contacts. I read statistics on how many contacts were required, on average, for a sale. All sorts of suggestions were given on how to create prospect lists.

In a short time, I started making calls on prospects. I soon realized that I was not cut out to be an insurance salesman. I sold a few policies, most of them to relatives or friends. But I didn't have the drive to call on total strangers and present a convincing sales pitch. Although Gene Smith was as helpful as he could have been, I soon gave it up. Two things came out of this experience: first, I learned that the insurance business could be a very lucrative business, if one were successful at it; and I learned about the different insurance plans and how they could be used, which was helpful to me in future years.

Following my fling at insurance, I got a job in the men's department of Leonard's Department Store. This was enjoyable enough but I took the job only as a stopgap until time for school to start.

During the summer, while I was wrestling with the question of what to study, I heard of a counseling service for veterans at Texas Christian University. I made an appointment to see what they could offer me in the way of career guidance. After several hours of taking various tests, I met with my counselor for the results.

"You show the strongest aptitude for social work," she reported.

"What does that mean?" I inquired.

"Well, you could work as counselor, community advisor, program planner, or program administrator. You might even consider a religious vocation. There are many ways to serve people and help with their problems."

"What's second?" I asked.

"You show a strong mechanical aptitude, which could point to engineering or one of the mechanical trades," she replied.

"I think I would like engineering."

I knew nothing about engineering and after further discussion I learned that there were several fields of engineering—mechanical, civil, electrical, chemical, etc.—to choose from. The counselor took out a book and read brief descriptions of the various fields of engineering. I recalled having seen men along the roads looking through some kind of instruments set up on tripods. I asked the counselor what type of engineer did that kind of work. She told me they were probably civil engineers. It looked to me like that would not be too difficult and you would be out of doors, which at that time appealed to me. So it was settled—I would study civil engineering.

In September 1946, I enrolled in NTAC (North Texas Agricultural College), located in Arlington, Texas. I was part of the large influx of World War II veterans that descended on campuses all across the country, thanks to the GI Bill. More than 2.5 million veterans became students in 1946 and 1947. College and University facilities and their faculties were completely overwhelmed. NTAC was a part of the Texas A&M University (then College) system and offered the freshman and sophomore years, only. Through the years the college has grown into a major university and is now the University of Texas at Arlington. Arlington is located midway between Dallas and Fort Worth. We continued to live in Fort Worth, and I commuted to Arlington daily.

The biggest problem I had, as a new freshman, was learning to study. It had been about eight years since I had been in school and even then I didn't do a very good job of studying. But this time it was different: I really meant business and was determined to spend as much time with the books as was necessary to succeed. That first semester I took a total of 13 credit hours, which included English, algebra, chemistry, and mechanical drawing. I spent every free hour during the day in the college library studying and in the evenings studying at home. The second semester, I took six courses for a total of 17 credit hours. In order to complete my degree as soon as possible, I enrolled in summer school, taking nine credit hours. At the end of the year I had completed 39 credit hours of classes with a grade average of B+. My diligence and hard work had paid off. I would say that was pretty good for a guy who just barely got through high school.

At the end of the summer session we moved to College Station and I transferred to Texas A&M University. By that time Darla was the personal secretary of Wyatt C. Hedrick, one of the foremost architects in Texas. Mr. Hedrick was very pleased with Darla's work (apparently he wasn't easy to work for) and tried every way to keep her in his employment. One of the options that we explored was for me to attend Rice Institute (now Rice University) in Houston so Darla could work in Hedrick's Houston office. After learning that Rice did not have summer school, I dropped this idea because I wanted to go year-round to complete my degree as soon as possible.

After much discussion over several days, Mr. Hedrick offered Darla a position as his personal secretary in his Houston Office. Mr. Hedrick divided his time between his Houston and Fort Worth offices. Part of the deal was that he would furnish Darla an apartment in Houston near his office during the week, would pay her transportation between College Station and Houston on weekends, and give her a very nice salary. After much agonizing, she accepted the offer.

Darla would leave the office early on Friday afternoons, and catch the train to College Station, arriving early in the evening. She would catch the return train to Houston early Monday morning. Under this arrangement she was away from home four nights a week but there were only three days that we didn't see each other. We lived with this arrangement for over a year.

While living in Fort Worth, Darla and I had become good friends with Dorothy and Tommy Evans. Tommy, like me, was a World War II veteran. Darla and Dorothy had met in church before either Tommy or I had been discharged. Tommy had enrolled in Texas A&M during the time I was going to NTAC. He and a friend had worked for a local landowner who had built several small one-bedroom houses a short distance from the campus. Darla and I bought one of these houses and moved in when I enrolled that fall. Dorothy and Tommy and their young son Tim were our neighbors and we developed a very close friendship which lasted beyond our days at Texas A&M.

During the first few months in College Station we didn't have a car, so we depended on rides with our neighbors, who were all married students. Automobile factories were just getting back into production from the war effort and cars were hard to buy because of the pent up demand. Through the connections of Mr. Hedrick, we were able to buy a new car at a very good price because he bought cars at fleet rates. In the fall of 1947 we became the proud owners of a new Dodge four-door sedan.

With Darla gone during the week, I had nothing to do but study. During that first year I spent many hours every week with the books, which paid off. Living alone, I was not much of a housekeeper. The neighbors said that they could always tell when Friday came; they would see the dust flying at our house, my cleaning it in preparation for Darla's arrival from Houston.

We continued for over a year with Darla commuting between College Station and Houston. My primary concern was my studies, so it wasn't too bad an arrangement for me. It was probably more difficult for Darla, being alone in the evenings in the big city. At that time, however, my cousin Wynon lived in Houston. She was married and had two children. Darla and Wynon became good friends and Darla would spend time with her and her family, which she enjoyed. Also, occasionally I would go to Houston for the weekend. It was less than 100 miles from College Station to Houston.

After a year of this, we decided that Darla should find a job in the College Station area so we could live a more normal life. Finding a job was not easy. The major employer in the area was the college and many veterans' wives were looking for jobs. The jobs that were available did not pay very well, certainly nothing compared to what Darla was getting with Wyatt C. Hedrick and Associates. After considerable looking, she "lucked" into a job with the Soil Conversation Service in Bryan, the larger town in the area which adjoined

College Station. This was a Civil Service job and paid much better than most secretarial jobs in the area. Darla terminated her employment with Mr. Hedrick and moved back to our little house at College Station.

Darla's time with the Hedrick firm was very good for her. The experience she gained there served her well in future years. During her employment with the firm, Mr. Hedrick was designing and building the Shamrock Hotel in Houston, which became a showpiece for Houston and the Southwest.

We had many good times the remaining time at Texas A&M. I studied hard and made good grades. We became very active in the First Baptist Church of Bryan and developed many good friendships. One couple I especially remember was Marion and Tom Claycomb. We had much in common. Tom was also a veteran and an engineering student, Marion worked as a secretary, and like us, they had no children. We became very close friends and spent much time together. During our Thanksgiving break in 1948 the four of us took a trip in our car to Monterey, Mexico. This was a real fun trip.

By the time we had had our Dodge a year, we realized that we had a "lemon." It was using oil badly. On one trip to Fort Worth and return I put five quarts of oil in the engine. The following morning I took it to the garage and was told the engine would need extensive overhauling, which would cost several hundred dollars. We decided to trade it in on another car.

We looked at many makes and models of cars and finally decided on a new 1949 Chevrolet convertible. It was white with a black top and red leather interior and was the first one like it in town. As we drove through the campus with the top down, we were the center of attraction. Tom and Marion were with us on our maiden cruise through the campus and they were as proud as we were.

Being in the civil engineering program, I had to take several required courses in steel and concrete structural design.

While I made good grades, I had a very strong dislike for these courses. One day in my junior year, while thumbing through the college catalogue, I discovered the Sanitary Option in Civil Engineering. In the Sanitary Option, the emphasis in the senior year was on courses in water treatment and distribution, wastewater collection and treatment, and municipal sanitation. I also discovered that if students choose the Sanitary Option, they didn't have to take any more structural courses. That looked good to me, so I chose the Sanitary Option. This decision, which had no more logic than my decision to enter civil engineering in the first place, was the start of my career in environmental engineering

Early in my senior year, I received notice that I had been elected into Tau Beta Pi, the most prestigious national honor society for engineering students. To be eligible, a student had to be in the upper twenty-five percent of his or her engineering class, scholastically. This recognition was one of the proudest occasions of my life.

By taking classes the year around, I graduated in January 1950, with a Bachelor of Science degree in Civil Engineering. I had accumulated 161 credit hours with a grade point average of 3.2. In addition to the required courses, I had taken elective courses in Bible, business law, and speech.

One accomplishment I was most proud of was my grades in mathematics courses. I had made an "A" in all college mathematics courses from algebra through calculus. This included perfect scores on all tests in the two semesters of calculus under "Dirty Shirt" Nelson, the terror of the math department. This was especially rewarding because of my miserable showing in high school math courses. Wouldn't Dr. Moore be surprised?

VII

My First Big Job

I thought that with my engineering degree and my good grades, I would have employers from all over the country knocking on my door, bidding for my services. Not so! Various companies sent recruiters to the campus every year to interview graduating seniors, but few came the year I graduated; those who came had few jobs to offer. Demand for entrance-level engineers was very low. I sent out numerous resumes and applications and received little interest in return. I was finally hired by the City of Abilene, Texas, in the Engineering Department, at a starting salary of $250 per month.

We rented a one-bedroom apartment in Abilene and settled in. For the first time in our marriage, we were living a "normal" married life. The first three years of our marriage I was in the Army. The next three-plus years I was in school. Now I had an eight-to-five job. We became active in the First Baptist Church and began to make new friends. The biggest adjustment we had was getting used to having our evenings and weekends free. For months, I had spent nearly every hour in the evenings and weekends studying. It took several weeks to get rid of the feeling that I was neglecting my studies in the evenings when we would relax or go to a movie.

My new job was exciting. As did most young civil engineering graduates of that era, I started out as party chief of a surveying crew. Abilene, about 50,000 population at that time, like most cities, was growing by leaps and bounds with new houses springing up in numerous subdivisions. My crew's job was to lay out new streets, water and sewer lines, sidewalks, and do other needed field work. I also inspected the construction done by contractors. It kept us hopping to keep up with the building, and I loved it.

The City Engineer, John Stiff, who was my boss, was about my age. He was a Navy veteran and had completed his civil engineering degree at Yale University during the war. He was a very nice guy, and he and wife, Harriet, and Darla and I became good friends. John could not stand to see one of his field parties or inspectors not busy. There were times when it was necessary to wait a few minutes on a contractor before our next task could be started. If John happened by during those times, he was not very understanding. He said he had rather we did something wrong than not do anything. I didn't agree with this, but we got along really well and became close friends. When I went to work in Abilene I took the place of Dave Cochran in the field party; he became the Assistant City Engineer. Dave had graduated from Texas A&M two years before I had and had started working for the City of Abilene at that time. Dave was also a Navy veteran, and he and John were in the Naval Reserve. They were both called to active duty during the Korean conflict. Dave was single and very often Darla and I would have him over for dinner. We became very good friends.

Abilene was a nice family town. It was the location of three colleges: the largest, Abilene Christian College, was operated by the Church of Christ; Hardin-Simmons, a Baptist college; and McMurry, a Methodist school. There were lots of sporting events and other cultural and entertainment activities. The many churches exerted a strong influence in the town.

When I went to work in Abilene, the City Manager was Austin P. Hancock. Mr. Hancock had been City Manager of Kerrville when I was growing up there. During those days I had no idea what a City Manager was or what one did, but I did remember that he had a large German shepherd dog that was always at his side. You never saw Mr. Hancock without him. Mr. Hancock didn't remember me, for I was just one of the kids of the town, but he remembered my father. Mr. Hancock took me under his wing and I learned a lot from him during the years we were together in Abilene. I remember one piece of advice that he gave me. He said, "When you have a problem that you don't know how to handle do nothing; very often it will go away—if it doesn't you have at least bought some time."

One day during my first year out of A&M, my field party was working in a new subdivision near the Abilene Christian College campus. I was dressed in work clothes, as usual, which were appropriate for that type of outdoor activity. I saw two young men approaching us who were obviously ACC Students. As they neared me, I heard one say, "You see that man," referring to me, "That's the reason I'm going to college, so I won't have to work like that." That was quite deflating to a newly graduated engineer, the ink on his diploma hardly dry. I guess I didn't look like what he thought a college graduate should look like.

My field party consisted of Charlie Allen the instrument man, Henry Hayes rodman/chainman, and another rodman/chainman whose name I don't remember. I doubt that Charlie had a high school education but he was a good instrument man. He was very accurate but he was as slow as molasses on a cold January morning. He could take 30 minutes to move a transit or level from one station to the next, a distance of 100 feet. His biggest problem was that he loved to talk. He would strike up a conversation with everyone who passed by, and nothing could move him until he finished what he had to say.

Like many not-so-educated people, Charlie wanted to prove his worth, and during the first months on the job he would test me at every opportunity. He wanted to show me that his years of experience outweighed the "book learning" of this young engineer. I went along with him without showing any concern and tried to cultivate his respect without its being obvious. I would ask him questions about surveying, for example, even though I knew the answers. In a short time we became good friends and respected each other's position. When Charlie accepted me, I knew I had made the grade.

After I had been in Abilene several months, the city started construction of a new 30-inch water supply line from Fort Phantom Hill Reservoir to the water treatment plant in town, a distance of about 10 miles. I was given the job of doing the fieldwork. My crew and I were on this job, almost full-time, for several months. We set line stakes and ran elevations over every inch of the route. The pipe was reinforced concrete cylinder, which was all laid to grade and had many special fittings that required extreme accuracy of layout. At the end of the job of several months' duration, carrying forward elevations over a distance of approximately ten miles, our elevation checked within 0.07 of a foot at the treatment plant. This was quite an accomplishment and a credit to Charlie's accurate work.

The engineering firm that designed and supervised the construction of the pipeline was Freeze and Nichols of Fort Worth. They were the city's engineers for most major projects during those years. I got to know Simon Freeze, the senior partner of the company, and a highly respected engineer who gave personal attention to the job. Mr. Freeze was a down-to-earth person and a brilliant engineer. He visited the job quite frequently and I enjoyed the time with him. He made a great impression on this young engineer. I always said that just following him around and listening to how he handled problems would be an education in itself. Years later, following his death, the American Society of Civil Engineers established the annual Simon Freeze Lecture in his honor. In 1983 I had the honor of presenting the lecture at the ASCE meeting in Cincinnati, Ohio, as the stand-in for the Deputy Assistant Administrator for Research and Development of the Environmental Protection Agency.

The first year in Abilene, Darla and I decided that it was time to start a family. Shortly after moving to Abilene, Darla had gone to work for the Soil Conservation Service, which she had also worked for while I was in A&M. We had been married seven years and with the war and my college behind us, we thought it time for her to take off to have children. Early in the morning of March 18, 1951, our son was born in Hendrix Memorial Hospital. We had had dinner at the home of some friends the night before and when we returned to our home at about 10 p.m. Darla informed me that she thought it was time to go to the hospital. Darla had had a normal pregnancy and her delivery went well. A healthy Curtis C. Harlin, III arrived at 3 a.m. that Sunday morning.

When mother and son came home from the hospital, they found that we had everything prepared: bassinet, diapers (cloth), clothes, powder, oil—the works. My mother came from Fort Worth for a few days, which was a big help. Before Curt's arrival—we always called him Curt to avoid confusion with his daddy and granddaddy—we had moved to a duplex just around the corner from where we previously lived. Mr. and Mrs. Evans, the parents of our good friend Tommy Evans from our days in Fort Worth and A&M, occupied the other side of the duplex. They took to Curt like he was their own grandson, and Mrs. Evans was a big help.

Curt was born with a good amount of hair, but in the months ahead he developed the most beautiful head of hair—copper colored with solid ringlets all over his head. He was a beautiful baby. Very often he would be mistaken for a girl, which annoyed his mother considerably. He was a good baby, slept well, had a good disposition, and was always healthy. We never had any trouble putting him to bed at night. We didn't own a rocking chair; when it was his bedtime we put him in his bed and he went to sleep without any fuss. Darla's mother and sisters thought we were awful, not rocking him. They were always used to rocking their babies to sleep.

Because of his good sleeping habits, we never had any problem with Curt when we went visiting. When he was a baby we would visit other couples of our age and circumstance in the evenings, and none of us would have baby sitters; we just took our babies with us. We had a portable baby bed, and when it was Curt's bedtime we put him in it in another room. We wouldn't hear anything from him until we were ready to go home. By contrast, other couples who had babies would disrupt the evening when their babies' bedtime came. The parents would rock them, try to put them down and invariably they would wake up crying. Everyone marveled at how good Curt was.

While I was in A&M I developed the desire to eventually teach in an engineering college. I realized that to be seriously considered for a teaching position, I needed graduate degrees. I contacted the Civil Engineering Department of Texas A&M about the possibility of financial assistance if I returned for graduate work. Dr. Wright, Department Chairman, told me he was sure I could have a teaching assistantship. This encouraged us to start making plans to go back to A&M at the start of the summer term of 1951.

Not long before we were to move back to College Station, I received a telephone call from Dr. Wright. He told me that Humble Oil Company (a predecessor of Exxon) gave two engineering scholarships to A&M each year, and that year one of them would be in the Civil Engineering Department. He explained that it would pay a stipend of $100 a month, tax free, and the recipient would have no duties. Was I interested? But definitely! So I returned to Texas A&M that summer for my master's degree on a Humble Oil Company scholarship.

We moved into a student apartment near the campus. It had two bedrooms and although the rooms were small, it was adequate for us. Curt had his own bedroom. The apartments were in what were formerly Army barracks from World War II. They were divided into eight apartments per building—

four up and four down. Ours was upstairs. There must have been as many as 20 or 30 of these buildings in the A&M married students' complex. Practically every college and university in the country had a similar area of surplus barracks for student housing. I still had enough GI Bill eligibility to cover a year. With that and my scholarship money from Humble, we did very nicely without Darla's working. Of course, our rent was only about $30 per month, including utilities.

In the master's degree program there was a choice of course work and research with thesis or additional course work without research and thesis. I choose the research and thesis option. I thought the research and writing experience would be valuable for me in a teaching career. I spent that summer in fulltime research. I selected as my research project a study of inlet structures in sedimentation basins and their effects on sedimentation efficiencies. This was important because sedimentation is one of the major processes in water treatment. There was already a pilot size sedimentation basin at the college treatment plant that I used in my research. In addition I constructed a Plexiglas laboratory model, which I used to evaluate different designs before trying them in the larger basin. It was fascinating work and I became quite knowledgeable about hydraulic flows through sedimentation basins.

The year at Texas A&M was very enjoyable for us. Curt started walking and was the center of our world. I worked and studied hard, but it was not as demanding as my undergraduate days. We became active again in the First Baptist Church of Bryan. Most of the students we knew when we were there before were gone, but we made new friends. The year passed very fast and in the spring of 1952 I received the Master of Science degree in Civil Engineering with minors in hydraulics and hydrology.

It was understood that the recipients of Humble Oil Scholarships were under no obligation to Humble Oil

Company after graduation, and neither was the company obligated to the students. However, Humble Oil had always offered their scholars jobs upon graduation; I was no exception. I was offered a job in Humble's Baytown, Texas, refinery in the Engineering and Inspection Department. At that time this refinery was one of the three largest in the world, the other two being located on the island of Aruba and at Bayway, New Jersey. I took the job because the starting salary was much higher than I could expect any other place. This turned out to be a mistake.

VIII

My Searching Years

We moved to Baytown after my graduation and settled in a nice single-family rental house. I was assigned to the cracking coils, probably the oldest and dirtiest unit in the refinery. I learned that this was the unit most new engineer-inspectors were first assigned to. My duties consisted of checking the records daily to be sure the operating conditions were in the prescribed range and planning and overseeing any required maintenance and repair work. I also assisted in the inspection of a new catalytic cracking unit that was under construction.

From the first week on the job I hated it. It was completely foreign to my training and experience, and I found it extremely boring. I felt that my education in civil and environmental engineering was completely wasted. Another thing that bothered me was the inspection work that I had to do on the new catalytic cracking unit. This unit was an open steel frame structure with pressure vessels and piping throughout; it was something over 20 stories high. When I was on that job it was like walking around in a skyscraper without any walls. I have always been afraid of heights, so after a day on this unit I was a nervous wreck. After three months I was ready to leave, but I had to have a job.

I had kept up with Dave Cochran, and through him I learned that the City of Abilene was in need of another engineer. I contacted the City Engineer and was hired. After being gone about a year and a half, we returned to Abilene. The experience in Baytown taught me a very valuable lesson:

never take a job strictly for the money. I learned that happiness and job satisfaction are also very important.

While I was away John Stiff and Dave Cochran had left Abilene. John had accepted the job of City Manager of Irving, Texas, and had taken Dave with him to be the City Engineer. I was sorry that they were no longer in Abilene, but their moves were good promotions for both of them. The new City Engineer in Abilene was Kenneth Ethridge, who had come from Wichita Falls, Texas. He was a very competent engineer but was quite different in his approach to things than was John. I enjoyed working with him, and we became good friends. Kenneth wanted to do more of the engineering in-house rather than through consulting engineers. Because of this, I gained much more experience with Kenneth than I would have with John.

At the time we moved back to Abilene, the city was embarking on a new airport project. I was hired to be the project engineer. The new airport was to be located across the highway from the old one and was to be completely new—runways, taxiways, fuel system, and terminal building. I was on the job from the first day when we started the layout until the completion of the project. This was one of the most interesting jobs I have ever had and was invaluable experience for a young engineer. I had the total responsibility for the project, which included layout, inspecting, testing, and reporting, involving earthwork, concrete work, building construction, electrical and plumbing work, and pipelines. It was like building a miniature city.

The airport was designed by Kenneth, and it was his baby. He visited the site often. He was also a pilot, and frequently we would go up in his plane to look at the project from the air. That job was certainly a rewarding experience. Not often is one so intimately involved with a project of that size from start to finish.

On October 16, 1952, our second child was born. Darla Ann was born in the same hospital and delivered by the same doctor as Curt had been 19 months before. She was a strong, healthy, little girl, and everything went well. Soon mother and daughter were home, and Curt was introduced to his little sister. We still had not acquired a rocking chair; we followed the same practice with Darla Ann we had with Curt—no rocking to sleep. She went to bed easily and slept regular hours from the beginning.

As Darla Ann grew, we found one difference in her and Curt—she seemed to be accident-prone. While growing up Curt didn't have serious accidents, but Darla Ann was frequently falling or having other mishaps, which left their marks on her. I remember when she was less than a year old and starting to pull up on things, trying to take a few steps, she fell against the edge of a door, hitting her forehead on the sharp edge and requiring an emergency trip to the doctor. To this day she carries a scar from this accident. That was the first of other accidents to follow.

Upon completion of the airport job, I took on the job of engineer for the Water and Sewer Department. This was a newly created job and was to prepare me for the job of superintendent of the department. Mr. L.A. Grimes had been superintendent for many years and was to retire soon. In the months ahead, as I tended to the engineering requirements of the department, Mr. Grimes groomed me for the day I would assume the duties he then had.

In 1955 I was appointed Superintendent to the Abilene Water and Sewer Department. The department had about 150 employees and included construction and operation of the distribution and collection systems, the treatment plants, the lakes, and the business office. By this time I was well-known by most of the employees; I had a good relationship with them. During the first months, I spent a lot of my time visiting the treatment plants, shops, and construction sites. I knew many of the employees by their first names.

Abilene was experiencing a phenomenal growth, as most cities did during that post-war era. Many new subdivisions were being developed and extending our water and sewer systems to serve them was a major challenge. It was a very interesting and challenging time for me. In 1954 I had completed the requirements for registration as a professional engineer and had become registered to practice engineering in the state of Texas. I became active in the professional engineering organizations and the American Water Works Association. I was becoming well-known around the state in municipal governmental circles.

In the mid-1950s while residing in Abilene we lived in a new housing development on the west side of town. A group from the First Baptist Church, where we were members, saw a need to organize and build a new Baptist Church in our fast-growing neighborhood. Those of us who lived in the neighborhood were encouraged to help in this endeavor. I became a charter member of the Pioneer Drive Baptist Church.

Shortly after its organization, when we had enrolled sufficient members, we needed to call a permanent pastor. (Local Baptist churches "call" their pastors, unlike many denominations' churches to which pastors are assigned by a bishop or by other means.) The calling of a new pastor is done through a pulpit committee elected by the church members. I was one of those elected to the pulpit committee to seek out the first pastor of Pioneer Drive Baptist Church.

The operation of a Baptist pulpit committee is an experience you would not believe unless you have served on one. Since my first experience at the Pioneer Drive Baptist Church, I have served on other pulpit committees. The committees usually range in size from five to ten members. Members are normally chosen to represent the different groups in the church—women, men, the Sunday school, the choir, etc.

The game plan is: identify prospective ministers; go to their churches, unannounced, and listen to them preach, with your identity kept a secret; narrow down the list of prospects to a few; and invite the top two or three candidates to your church to give a "trial" sermon and look over the church. This last step is referred to as inviting the preacher to your church "in view of a call." A call is issued to a preacher when the congregation votes to call one of the candidates as its pastor. Sometimes when a preacher is called to a church he doesn't accept the call, for various reasons. This does not happen very often, but when it does, the process must start over again or one of the other candidates may be called.

As soon as the makeup of a pulpit committee is announced, it seems like every church member has their favorite preacher that the committee must look at. In a very short time, the list of prospects can be longer than the committee could possibly get around to in a reasonable period of time. Some on the list are obviously losers. The trick is to reduce the list to a manageable number.

There is usually the little old lady who has a nephew who, in her mind, is ideal for the job. It turns out that he is a high school drop-out, the only theology training he has was taken by correspondence from a questionable Bible institute on the west coast, and he has a very bad speech impediment. Every time you see the lady, you have to make up a reasonable-sounding excuse why the committee has not seen her nephew yet. This goes on until every time you see the lady coming you realize you have urgent business in the opposite direction.

Being a member of a pulpit committee is not an easy job. It can require lots of traveling, many meetings, and a lot of time and patience. Even when everything goes smoothly, it usually takes several months to complete the job. I have known of churches that took over a year to call a pastor. The longer it takes the more difficult the task becomes. Divisive differences of opinion can develop within the committee, factions can develop within the congregation, and long-term animosities can be created. There must be a better way, but after all the years of Baptist history, no one has come forward with an acceptable alternative.

The biggest farce of the entire process is the "secret" visits to the churches to hear the prospective preachers. No one in their own church is supposed to know where the committee members are going, and certainly the preacher being looked at is not supposed to know. The fact is that the itinerary of the pulpit committee is the best known secret in most churches. It could hardly be more widely known if it were announced in the Sunday Bulletin.

Usually two or three committee members will go together for the first screening visits, although sometimes one member will go alone. When committee members visit a prospect's church, the idea is to blend in and not attract any attention. If more than one committee member is on the mission, they never enter the church together and never sit together. All of these precautions are usually wasted. All Baptist preachers have some kind of natural radar for locating and identifying people in their congregation who are not members. They can be sorted into several classifications: out-of-town visitors on vacation, relatives of members, those who are in town to attend conventions or on business, disgruntled members of other local churches looking for a new church, and members of pulpit committees. I have had preachers say to me after a service, "We had a pulpit committee visiting us this morning." I would ask, "How do you know that?" "I just know," he would reply with a grin.

One sure way for a pulpit committee member to give away his or her identity is to not fill out a visitor's card. Most Baptist Churches make a big deal about visitors in their services. At some point, early in the service, all visitors are given a saccharine, mushy welcome. Very often they are asked to stand or raise their hands, "...so our members can identify you and get to know you after the service." While their hands are still up or they are still standing, the ushers pass down the isles and hand them a visitor's card. The

114

pastor, or whoever is doing the greeting, will urge them to fill out the card and drop it in the collection basket later in the service. The card asks for information about them which is to help the church, "...minister to your needs."

A sure way of identifying yourself as a member of a pulpit committee is to not fill out the visitor's card. Everyone knows that the only people on earth who do not want to be identified in a Baptist Church service are pulpit committee members. As soon as the pastor, or those sitting around you, sees you stick the card in your pocket or purse, or leave it on the pew when you leave, you are branded a member of a pulpit committee.

Our Pioneer Drive Baptist Church committee had a fairly manageable number of prospects from the beginning. Several things made our job easier. First, we were a young church made up of people who had not been together for long and, consequently, did not have a lot of old hang-ups and set opinions. We were more open than an older congregation would have been. Because we were small in number, the number of suggestions we received was comparatively small. We were an enthusiastic group and were anxious to have a pastor and ready to give him our support.

In due time, we called our first pastor, Edward Laux. He was pastor of a church in McGregor, Texas, which is near Waco. He and his wife, Dorothy, were truly a God-send. They had no children and really worked as a team. We became very good friends in the months ahead.

Shortly after calling our pastor we launched into a building program. I was also on the building committee. The trials and tribulations of a building committee member can dwarf those of a pulpit committee member. Suffice it to say, we completed the church's first permanent building which was not elaborate, but adequate. We had plenty of property for expansion which, after I left, would accommodate another larger unit.

It was not very long before the church needed to elect deacons. We had deacons in the congregation who had been a part of the original membership, but as the congregation was growing by leaps and bounds there was a need for additional deacons to help the pastor carry out the programs of the church.

Deacons in Southern Baptist Churches are elected by the congregation. They are elected for life—once a deacon always a deacon. Most Baptist churches have some kind of rotation system for deacons. A certain number of deacons are active deacons, often for three-year terms, and are responsible for the ministries and business of the church. Those not on the active list are still expected to perform duties of ministry but do not have specific assignments. Others from the deacon body rotate to the active list at the end of a deacon's active term. This spreads the labor and puts on the shelf some of the dead wood that always develops as the deacon body ages.

As I recall, there were three deacons in the congregation in the beginning, and it was decided to add three new deacons. The system calls for nominations from any member of the church. The qualifications for deacons follow those given in I Timothy 3: 8-13. At the end of the nomination period, those nominated are interviewed by the pastor, chairman of the deacons, or someone else appointed for that duty. The candidates are quizzed on their qualifications and beliefs and asked if elected would they faithfully serve. Those who survived these interviews are voted on by the congregation.

I was elected one of the new deacons of the Pioneer Drive Baptist Church. No one can accept the responsibilities of a deacon without a feeling of unworthiness. If he feels otherwise I would doubt that he should accept the position. The job should seek the man, not the man the job. I felt a deep sense of inadequacy, but if the congregation was willing to honor me with the position I would do my best, with the Lord's help. I was ordained a deacon at Pioneer

Drive Baptist Church January 9, 1955. It is an humbling experience to realize you have joined that holy body that was started with the setting aside of Stephen, Philip, Prochorus, Nicanor, Timon, Parmenas, and Nicolaus in the first century, just a few years after the crucifixion of Christ (Acts 6: 1-6). I was also proud to follow in the footsteps of my grandfather Dodd who faithfully served as a deacon in years past.

In 1957 Dave Cochran resigned as City Engineer of Irving to take a job elsewhere. I got a call from John Stiff asking me to take Dave's place as city engineer. This looked like a logical stepping-stone in my career so I accepted the position. Once again I was working for John Stiff, and once again I followed in Dave's footsteps.

As city engineer, I had broader responsibilities than I had in Abilene. I not only oversaw all the engineering activities of the city—design and construction of the water system, sewer system, streets, sidewalks, etc.—I also had responsibility for the electrical, plumbing, and building permitting and inspection, and city planning.

At that time, Irving was the fastest growing city in the nation, in its population class (about 50,000). It was impossible to keep up with the needs for water and sewer lines, streets, and other services. When I worked in Irving, there was some open space between it and Dallas, Grand Prairie, Arlington, and the other small towns situated in the Dallas-Fort Worth area. Today, one cannot tell where Dallas, Grand Prairie, Arlington, and Irving end and the next city begins. It is just one huge metropolis. Texas Stadium, home of the Dallas Cowboy football team, is located in Irving. Part of the large Dallas-Fort Worth International Airport extends into the Irving city limits. It is not the growing small city of 50,000 population that I worked in over 50 years ago.

I had hardly gotten settled in Irving when I received an offer from the City of Waco, Texas, to head their water and sewer department. This was a very attractive opportunity, one I had not expected. Waco was a city of about 100,000 population located on the Brazos River in central Texas. It was a good place to raise a family. Professionally, it was an opportunity of a lifetime. It was a difficult decision, especially after being in Irving such a short time, but we finally decided to move to Waco.

In Waco we purchased a nice three-bedroom home in a nice quite neighborhood. We had no trouble making new friends and soon became involved in a Baptist Church. Waco is the home of Baylor University. The university and the many Baptist churches in the city had a strong influence. In my job I was in a position to become acquainted with many of the business and community leaders of the city. My predecessor had been very active in community affairs, and I was expected to follow his example. It seemed that we had really found a home in Waco, a place where we could live for many years and see our children grow up.

The job was very challenging. The city, like most cities at that time, was experiencing phenomenal growth, and the growth placed great demands on the public utilities. To add to these problems, when I went there the area was going through a period of below normal rainfall, which increased the water usage, thus stressing the water system. Waco depended on the Brazos River for its water supply, and because of the low rainfall, the flow in the river was significantly reduced. The first year I was there, we had numerous problems, including low water pressure and high demand. In spite of the water restrictions that we imposed, in one section of the city there was actually no water from the taps for a few hours in the afternoons during the hot summer. These conditions did not make the new water superintendent's life very pleasant. Commenting on all of our water problems at a staff meeting one day, our city attorney jokingly observed that the city hadn't had any water problems before Curtis came.

Settled in our new home with a nice fenced backyard, we decided that the children should have a dog; we bought the cutest little boxer puppy. We fell in love with him and the children really enjoyed him. The trouble with boxer pups is that they don't stay cute little pups; they grow into big boxer dogs, fast. Before long he was twice his original size. Darla Ann was only one or two years old, and soon the pup was so large, that when playing with her, he would knock her down and she would lie on the ground screaming and crying until she was rescued. In a short time we decided the boxer had to go. We proceeded to find him a good home in the country. Moral: Don't buy a boxer pup for a one-year-old child.

As interesting and challenging as my job was, and in spite of our family enjoying living in Waco, after a couple of years I became restless again. I could not get the idea of teaching out of my mind. I learned of an opening in the Civil Engineering Department of the University of Alabama. I applied for the job and was accepted with the rank of assistant professor. Once again, I resigned from a very secure position, we sold our house, and we were on our way to Tuscaloosa, Alabama.

The Civil Engineering Department was small, having only six full-time faculty members. The department chairman was nearing retirement and spent only as much time in his office as he absolutely had to. He was a very nice man but had no interest in anything new and gave very little help to this young assistant professor. Two other faculty members were also much older and had been there for many years. The other two faculty members were about my age but had had several years of teaching experience. The faculty was evenly divided between young and old members, and I soon realized that there was a wide gulf between the two groups. All of the older faculty members did private consulting and taught only the minimum number of hours, while the three of us younger members carried the load.

By the end of the academic year I was completely disillusioned and decided to look for something else. I took a summer job with a Dallas engineering firm that was building a sewerage system in Sweetwater, Texas. I was hired to be the resident engineer for the firm. Since the job was to last only through the summer, we decided that Darla and the children would spend the summer with my parents who by then had bought a farm near Alvarado, Texas, and had built a nice new house. The children loved the farm with the cattle, pigs, and chickens. I rented a small apartment in Sweetwater. Some weeks I would drive to Alvarado for the weekend. A couple of times Darla and the children came to Sweetwater for a few days. I had jokingly told the children that the water in Sweetwater was actually sweet. The first time they visited me, I slipped some sugar in the glass of water I gave them. After tasting it, they exclaimed: "The water is really sweet; we thought Daddy was just joking." The next time they had a drink of the water, they knew I had been joking.

As the end of the job neared, I began to look around for a permanent job; I was confident I would have no problem. By the time the job ended, I had not located anything. I looked for employment fulltime, concentrating in the Dallas-Fort Worth area. I knew people in several engineering firms in that area from my days in Abilene, Irvine, and Waco. I visited them and also others that I got leads on, but I was unsuccessful. School started and we enrolled Curt in the Alvarado school system. I continued my search for a job.

From some source, I learned that the city of Tulsa, Oklahoma, was looking for a Deputy Director for their water and sewer department. I sent my resume to the personnel department and was invited for an interview. The director, William Jewell, interviewed me and also introduced me to the water commissioner and other city officials. I left Tulsa to return to Alvarado without a clue as to what they thought of me. Everyone I talked to was very courteous and interested but very noncommittal.

Several days passed without any word from Tulsa. I had just about written them off when I received a telephone call from Mr. Jewell. He was very formal in his conversation, telling me that the selection committee had decided on me, and wanted to know when I could start. I didn't want to appear too eager, so I told him I could probably arrange my affairs to report on a certain date. Actually, I could have been there the next day. I had been without a job for three months and was getting desperate. I made many moves during my career, but that was the only time I left a job without having another job to go to. It wasn't the smartest thing I ever did.

The move to Tulsa was very trying. We had moved our household goods from Alabama, and having no permanent place to live, we had stored them in my parents' barn. Funds being short, our move to Tulsa was the hard way—by U-Haul.

We rented a three-bedroom house in the Brookside area of Tulsa, not far from my new office. It was only a block from the Arkansas River. We were only two blocks from the elementary school that Curt attended. We became active in the Brookside Baptist Church and quickly made new friends.

Tulsa was a city of over 300,000 population, and the water and sewer systems were much larger operations than I had dealt with in my previous jobs. Under the Director there were two Deputy Directors, one for operations and one for engineering and planning. This was a recent change in organization, and I was the first Deputy Director for Operations. Bud Wheatley, who had previously been the only deputy director, was the Deputy Director for Engineering and Planning.

As Deputy Director for Operations, I was responsible for most of the department's day-to-day functions. I was in charge of the Lakes and Flow Line Division, the Treatment Division, the Maintenance Division, and the Construction Division. These divisions had a total of about 350 employees. The Deputy Director for Engineering and Planning had the Engineering Division and a small planning group totaling about 50 employees. I had good division heads, which helped me get my feet on the ground fairly quickly. I loved the job and began to make improvements in the way we did business. The operation had not kept up with new methods and materials, so there was much to be done.

Tulsa was a lovely city. It had beautiful parks, entertainment facilities, stores and shopping areas, and many churches. It had a good school system and was very progressive and business-oriented. We made friends easily.

Curt started taking piano lessons in Tulsa. After a while we asked his piano teacher if she would also take Darla Ann. She said that she had never had such a young student—Darla Ann was only four years old—but she would give it a try. Soon, by accident, the teacher discovered that Darla Ann had perfect pitch. This was an exciting discovery for the teacher as well as for Darla Ann's parents. With our permission, the teacher took Darla Ann to the University of Tulsa to demonstrate her talent to one of the music classes. Curt and Darla Ann both did well and seemed to have considerable musical talent.

The second year that we lived in Tulsa, Darla Ann started to kindergarten in the same school as Curt attended. Curt had started in first grade while we were in Alvarado, but we had moved to Tulsa a few months into the school year. Curt had finished the first grade in Tulsa. We lived only a couple of blocks from their school, which made it very convenient for us.

One day while at work, I received a call from Darla telling me that Darla Ann had fallen out of a tree and had broken her arm. She was calling from the doctor's office. Later that morning Darla brought Darla Ann to my office. She was so embarrassed with her arm in a cast and being held in a sling, that she didn't want any of those in my office to see her. This was another of her many accidents.

I couldn't get the thought of teaching out on my mind. Even after the disappointing experience at the University of Alabama, I still felt a strong desire for an academic career. I also realized that in order to teach in a first class engineering school, a doctorate was essential. This led me to start inquiring about doctoral programs in various universities. Universities that I considered were the University of Florida, Johns Hopkins University, Cal Tech, and Washington University. The most encouraging response I received was from Washington University in St. Louis, Missouri. We finally made a visit to Saint Louis and were very pleased with what we saw. The big question was: How would I support my family? I was 40 years old, had a wife and two young children. I also had a very good job with a promising future. Mr. Jewel had confided in me, when I told him I was thinking about leaving, that he would retire in about two years and he was sure that I would be the next Director of Utilities for the City of Tulsa.

Dr. Ryckman, head of the Environmental Engineering Program at Washington University, was optimistic about my being able to get a U.S. Public Health Service Fellowship. After reading the instructions and information about applying for a fellowship, I was not as optimistic as he was. I didn't meet any of the criteria for eligibility—I was over-age, had too many years of work experience, and had been out of school too long. Nevertheless, I filled out the application and mailed it to the Public Health Service. Much to my surprise, after what seemed a very long wait, I was notified that I had been chosen to receive a fellowship which would pay for my tuition, books and supplies, and a stipend that, if we were careful, we could live on. Dr. Ryckman was successful in getting us into on-campus student housing, although there were others ahead of us. So I resigned my secure position in Tulsa, loaded our belongings in another U-Haul and headed for St. Louis to start my studies in the summer of 1960 at Washington University.

Our move to St. Louis required some adjustments. Our house was again Army quarters from World War II. This time it consisted of two 6-man huts joined together and divided into a living room, kitchen with eating area, a bathroom, and two bedrooms. All of the rooms were very small as the house had only a total of about 500 square feet. I recalled when I worked as a carpenter at Fort Sill, before going into the Army, I helped build hundreds of these huts. A number of these houses were located in a wooded area on the edge of the campus. The construction left much to be desired. The walls were plywood with no insulation, and at night the light from inside the house could be seen outside through the cracks in the walls. But the price was right—about $30 per month, including all utilities.

I had been out of school for about eight years, and I soon found that the change from an eight-to-five job to being a student required some serious adjusting. I had to learn how to study all over again. One big change was that during the intervening years we had entered the computer age. When I was at Texas A&M students didn't have access to a computer unless they were involved in a special project. This had changed and many of the students in my class had access to a computer. I remember spending hours on design problems that other students, much younger than I, would crank out on a computer in a very short time.

Dr. Ryckman was my major professor; we decided that I would take my minor in chemistry. Analytical chemistry classes that I took in the department were not too bad, but the courses I had to take in the Chemistry Department were more challenging. I found organic chemistry fascinating; it has order, which made it fairly easy for me to master, but it required a lot of memorizing. Physical chemistry was a different story. When I picked up the textbook at the bookstore and thumbed through it, I thought I had the wrong book—it looked like an advanced mathematics book. I really struggled with physical chemistry.

By the end of my first semester, I had decided on my research topic. One major problem in many public water systems is objectionable tastes and odors. This is especially true of systems that have surface sources—rivers and lakes. I decided on a project to identify and characterize the organic materials that cause the tastes and odors in our water supplies. I used, as a source of water in the study, the Missouri River, which flowed into the Mississippi River at St. Louis and was convenient to access.

I spent hours in the laboratory analyzing water samples. Also, an important part of the project was characterizing the odors from my samples. The standard way of doing this, was utilizing a panel to determine the types of odors from different concentrations. I used my classmates for my panels. With some practice, a person can become quite good at identifying and evaluating odors.

During my time at Washington University there were about 15 graduate students in the environmental engineering program. They were about equally divided between doctoral and masters' candidates. The doctoral candidates had the choice of going for the Doctor of Philosophy or the Doctor of Science degree. The requirements for the degrees were essentially the same, but if you went the Ph.D. route your committee was from the College of Liberal Arts. For those taking the Sc.D. route their committee was from the Sever Institute, which was the home of graduate studies in engineering and science. I chose the Sc.D.

I had heard horror stories about students who had chosen the Ph.D. Their committee could be composed of faculty members from the departments of English, history, art, philosophy, and other liberal arts departments—disciplines that had no relation to engineering. Committee members for the Sc.D. candidates would have engineering and science backgrounds. Two of my classmates, that I remember, wanted to have Ph.D. after their names. When it came time for them to defend their theses before their committees, I am sure they would have gladly changed to the Sc.D. program. One of these classmates was so overcome by the experience that he passed out and had to go to the emergency room

The very minimum time required for completing a doctoral program at Washington University was two years, going full-time. Few students completed the program in two years. The course work was not the problem; it was the research and production of a thesis that could bog you down. I was determined that I would finish in two years. I was 40 years old and had a family. I felt that I could not spend any more time than that away from a normal life.

I completed most of my course work during the first year. My second year was devoted primarily to research and writing my thesis. I would spend the mornings in the laboratory, and after lunch would go back to the laboratory or to the library, where I would work until dinnertime. After dinner—back to the laboratory or the library. During the last few months, when I was writing the thesis and doing only confirmatory laboratory work, I worked at the laboratory through the night, until early morning. I would arrive home and get two or three hours of sleep before the family awoke and Curt and Darla Ann were off to school. I would then return to my writing until lunch. After lunch I would take a nap before returning to my writing. Finally, my long hours and hard work paid off—I had completed my research and my thesis. The defense of my thesis before my committee went well, and I had completed my Doctor of Science degree in two years—almost unheard of at Washington University.

In spite of my hard work and long hours, our two years in St. Louis, living in substandard housing on the campus of Washington University, were enjoyable. We found time to visit and enjoy the sights in the area, including Forest Park and the renowned St. Louis Zoo. In the summers we went to the fabulous outdoor Muny Opera. The housing area that we lived in was in the Clayton School district; therefore the children attended a Clayton school. Clayton was a very wealthy suburb of St. Louis and had an excellent school system.

While we were in St. Louis Curt was in the third grade. One day we received a call from his teacher requesting that we see her about Curt's behavior. The next day when I met with the teacher, she told me that she adored Curt but sometimes he was disruptive in the class because of his clever antics. As an example she cited an instance when she asked the class to tell her words that had more than one meaning. Curt immediately raised his hand and said that the word "vest" had more than one meaning. He explained, "There is the vest that you wear," then he continued with a long story about people moving in covered wagons out to the "vild, vild, vest." His teacher said he was always coming up with something like that, and while she thought he was very clever and imaginative, and it was all she could do to keep from laughing, his stories were disruptive. I told her I would have a word with him.

With much relief I received my Doctor of Science degree in Environmental Engineering from Washington University in May 1962.

IX

At the University of Wisconsin

By the time I graduated I had accepted a job with the University of Wisconsin as an assistant professor of civil engineering. The job would not start until the fall semester so we had the entire summer to enjoy ourselves. We planned an extensive trip of the New England states and the eastern provinces of Canada. We had camping equipment and planned to do a lot of camping along the way. Curt and Darla Ann were at the age that they thought that was a real adventure.

Our first major stop was Washington, D.C. We stayed there three or four days and saw the monuments, museums, and great buildings. We stayed in a downtown hotel so we would be near everything. We walked everywhere. By the time we returned to our hotel in the evenings, we were worn out. It was a great experience for the children—and their parents too.

Leaving Washington we spent time in Baltimore, Annapolis, Philadelphia, and New York seeing the sights. We continued on through Connecticut, Massachusetts, Vermont, New Hampshire, and Maine. In Bangor, Maine, we met Otis Sproul and his wife Dorothy and their two sons. Otis had been a classmate of mine at Washington University, had graduated a semester before I had, and was teaching at the University of Maine. Their sons were about the age of Curt and Darla Ann; we had been close friends while in St. Louis. We had planned our trip to meet them in Bangor and then travel in Canada together. They enjoyed camping too.

Our first stop in the province of New Brunswick was Fundy National Park. Our campsite was on a high bluff overlooking the Bay of Fundy and was spectacular. The bay's fast moving tide is the highest in the world, sometimes reaching 70 feet. We spent several days in the park exploring the surrounding area. A not-so-enjoyable event was rain. Several of the days, while we were there, we had rain. This was only the beginning of rains that followed us through Canada and back into the U.S.A. This was not a welcomed experience for four sleeping in a small tent. Following our time in the southern part of New Brunswick, we crossed over into Nova Scotia. This was a beautiful area, its Scottish influence adding to its charm. After a couple of days we caught the ferry to Prince Edward Island, Canada's smallest province. We had planned to stay only one day, but we missed the last ferry of the day to New Brunswick and had to stay an extra night. Our most lasting memory of Prince Edward Island is the rain: from the time we arrived until our departure it came down constantly, sometimes in torrents. Needless to say, we spent the nights in a motel. The children were fascinated by the stacks of lobster traps on the wharfs. They had never seen them before.

The next morning, after our unscheduled overnight, we took the ferry to New Brunswick. We traveled the northern part of New Brunswick, stopping several places, and entered the province of Quebec. Paralleling the St. Lawrence River, we reached the city of Quebec. We spent several days in the city—a fascinating place. By this time we had been traveling with the Sprouls about two weeks, and it was time for them to head toward home.

We continued south through Montreal and entered the state of New York. We visited the Finger Lakes region of New York and continued through western Pennsylvania, Ohio, Indiana, and Illinois to St. Louis. We had been gone six weeks and had visited about a dozen states and four Canadian provinces. Our intention had been to do mostly camping, but because rain seemed to follow us everywhere we went, we probably spent more nights in motels than in our tent. When we returned home, I let it be known that any area of the country that was having a drought could call me and I would come and put up our tent and guarantee them rain. I had no takers. Now we were back home facing the challenge of moving to Madison, Wisconsin.

We made a trip to Madison, and after spending several days looking at housing, we bought a fairly new home in a nice subdivision. It was located within a couple of blocks of a new elementary school, convenient for the children, and not too far from the university campus. It would be a big step up from the substandard housing we had lived in for two years on the Washington University campus. We had managed our finances fairly well while I was in school, but of course we had not been able to accumulate much. The down payment on our house in Madison almost depleted what assets we had. Also, our six-week trip had cut into our resources; consequently, we moved to Madison, again the hard way, by U-Haul.

We had two or three weeks before the university started, which gave us time to get settled and get Curt and Darla Ann enrolled in their school. I checked in with the university and learned where my office was located and what my class assignments were. I would teach undergraduate courses in water supply and water and wastewater treatment design. I obtained the textbooks and spent a lot of time in preparing lesson plans and lectures.

The first Sunday we were in Madison we visited and joined the only Southern Baptist Church in town, which was only a few blocks from our new home. The congregation was small but enthusiastic. Most of the members, like we, were transplants, many having some connection with the university. There were other Baptist churches in Madison of different associations, but this was mission country for the Southern Baptists, and there were few of us. An incident that illustrates how few we were, and how misunderstood we were, occurred with the young daughter of our pastor. One day in her school the students were telling the class what church they went to. I don't know why this was being discussed in a public school; even then there was a strong feeling about injecting religion into the classroom. When it came the pastor's daughter's turn, she correctly stated that she went to the Southern Baptist Church. The teacher immediately corrected her saying that she surely didn't go to the Southern Baptist Church because that was a Negro church. The pastor's daughter insisted that she was right. She went home that afternoon quite upset because of the experience. Her mother called the teacher and put her straight about the Southern Baptist denomination.

We became very much involved with our church: I was put on the Board of Deacons, I sang in the choir, and Darla and I both taught Sunday School classes. Our pastor was a very nice young man, originally from Missouri I think. We became very close friends with him and his attractive wife. She was very talented and was involved in a local television show.

Once school started we all became very busy. I spent much time preparing my lessons, being the first time I taught those courses, but I thoroughly enjoyed it. The children enjoyed their school, and Darla spent time with church work and getting acquainted with the area. We had not been in Madison very long before winter arrived and we had our first snow. We had snow in St. Louis, but nothing like we had in Madison. The children loved it, especially Curt. He would stay out in it, going up and down the hills on his shed or building a snowman, until he was finally made to come in the house. His pants would be frozen stiff, but he didn't seem to mind it. Darla Ann, on the other hand, knew when she had had enough. When we announced that we were moving to Wisconsin, people would say, "The cold won't bother you; it's a dry cold." Believe me, when it is minus 30° it is cold, dry or not!

As mentioned earlier, Curt always had a great imagination and keen sense of humor. When I was teaching at the

University of Wisconsin, I was commonly addressed as Dr. Harlin. One day one of Curt's buddies said, "Curt, what kind of doctor is your dad?" Curt's reply, "He's one of those doctors that can't do you any good."

The first year we were in Madison my mother and father came from Texas to spend Christmas with us. I remember that the temperature Christmas morning was 32° below zero. This was such an experience for my folks that my father insisted that I take their picture in our front yard standing knee-deep in snow.

The school year passed very quickly, and I thoroughly enjoyed my teaching job. I found the other faculty members to be very congenial and helpful, unlike the ones I had met during my year at the University of Alabama. My office was in the Old Hydraulics Building on Lake Mendota across the street from the Student Union Building. I was on the lakeside, and I could look out my window at a beautiful view of the lake. In the summer the lake would be covered with sailboats, with swimmers in the reserved area in front of the Student Union. In the winter you could see iceboats and fishermen in their shelters fishing through the ice. Summer or winter it was a magnificent sight.

At that time the University of Wisconsin was one of the most liberal campuses in the country, although I didn't give it much thought when I was there. One of its claims to fame was that it was one of the few universities that allowed beer to be sold on campus. The Rathskiller in the Student Union was where students could hang out and have a beer. During the Vietnam conflict, the campus was the sight of violent demonstrations, but this was after I had left.

I had no summer classes that first year, so it was decided that the family would take a tour of the west. We bought a camping trailer that, when the top was opened, could accommodate the four of us nicely. Our first big stop was the Badlands of South Dakota. The wind- and water-sculptured terrain is spectacular. Next we visited the Black Hills and the

132

famous presidential sculptured mountain. The Black Hills area is beautiful, and with its tree-covered hills is such a contrast to its neighbor, the badlands. Turning north we visited the badlands of North Dakota and the state capitol. The North Dakota badlands are exciting but not as extensive as those in South Dakota. Continuing west we arrived at Yellowstone National Park. We spent several days there and enjoyed fishing for cutthroat trout in Yellowstone River. We were gone on this trip about three weeks and camped every day, unlike our Canadian trip the previous summer.

Our home in Madison did not have a car garage, which I sorely missed during the previous winter. On our return home I made plans to build the much-needed garage. I designed a single-car garage with extra width for workshop and storage. I acquired the necessary building permit, staked it out, and set the forms for the concrete slab. I enlisted the help of one of my colleagues to help me with the concrete pour. I ordered the concrete to be delivered early in the morning. By the time the concrete truck arrived I had seen nothing of my helper. When a driver has a load of concrete, he doesn't want to stand around waiting while the mixer continues to rotate. He wants to get his load delivered. There was nothing to do but start pouring the concrete without my expected helper. Fortunately, the driver was very accommodating—he helped me spread the concrete. Once the concrete was poured into the forms, it had to be troweled and finished which I started. I worked all day and late into the night. Leveling and spreading a slab the size of a garage is not a one-man job. By the time I finished, the concrete had begun to set up so the last area that I finished was not very smooth. Nevertheless, I finished it, and no one but me would ever notice the flaws.

The head of the Environmental Engineering Section of the department, Jerry Rohlick my boss, was a very likable guy, and he was a big help during my first year at Wisconsin. He was highly regarded by his associates throughout the country and was very active in professional organizations. He was on a review board of the U.S. Public Health Service that reviewed grant applications, and was called to Washington often for their meetings. In his absence I was the substitute for his classes. Early in my second year, Jerry took leave and taught for several months at a university in India leaving me with his classes. Being the senior faculty member, his teaching load was not large; nevertheless, I had a fairly heavy load the first semester of that year. I profited a great deal by my association with Jerry as he was so well known and respected in the profession.

I, like most Americans, remember very well where I was when I heard the news that President Kennedy had been assassinated. Our house in Madison had a full basement but it was unfinished. I had taken on the project of finishing it and making it a recreational room. I was working in the basement November 22, 1963, when Darla came down with the news that she had just heard on the radio that President Kennedy had been shot.

The President and First Lady were in Dallas and were riding in an open-air limousine, with Texas Governor John Connelly and his wife, when shots from a nearby warehouse killed the president and wounded Governor Connelly. They were rushed to Parkland Memorial Hospital but Kennedy was pronounced dead upon arriving there. The assassin was determined to be Lee Harvey Oswald who never stood trial. While he was being moved from one jail to another he was shot and killed by a nightclub owner named Jack Ruby. Ruby was convicted of murder and died in prison in 1967.

Vice President Johnson was in a car behind the president in the Dallas motorcade when the president was shot. He was sworn in as president on *Air Force One* as the plane sat on the tarmac at Love Field in Dallas.

Early in the second semester, I received a telephone call from a Dr. Leon Weinberg, who identified himself as the chief of the water research division of the U. S. Public Health Service. He explained that congress had authorized the building of seven regional water research laboratories, and he was responsible for staffing these new facilities. He asked if I would be interested in the job of research director of one of the laboratories. I knew who Dr. Weinburg was, because of his position in the Public Health Service, but I had had no association with him and had never met him. It turned out that my major professor at Washington University, Dr. Ryckman, had given him my name and recommended me. This call had come as a big surprise, and my response to Dr. Weinburg was that I was perfectly happy at the University of Wisconsin, and I was not looking for a job.

In the next few weeks I had several calls from Dr. Weinburg. Each time he would give more information about the proposed laboratories and their missions. The legislation authorizing the laboratories had specified that laboratories be built to serve water research needs on a regional basis and that they should be located near universities. Several locations had been selected including Corvallis, Oregon, Ada, Oklahoma, Athens, Georgia, and Fairbanks, Alaska, and the research director's job was still unfilled at most of these locations. I was flattered that I would be considered for one of these jobs, but I was still not convinced that I should leave Wisconsin. Finally, Dr. Weinburg invited me to visit him in Washington to discuss the jobs. I accepted, thinking it wouldn't do any harm, and the trip, at government expense, would be nice.

I took an afternoon flight to Washington and spent the night in a downtown hotel; my meeting with Dr. Weinburg was the next morning. Dr. Weinburg was very cordial and easy to talk to. He introduced me to the staff and I felt very comfortable with those I met. Dr. Weinburg didn't provide much new information, as he had been over much detail during our several telephone conversations. The aura of Washington, D.C.—the huge buildings, the monuments, the capital building—has always filled me with awe. The thought of being even a small part of this magnificent and powerful governmental structure must have weakened my resolve to stay in Wisconsin. I found myself, for the first time, considering one of the jobs that was being offered me. I began to focus my attention on the laboratory that was planned for Ada, Oklahoma; none of the other locations appealed to me. My family had strong roots in Oklahoma: my mother and father had been raised there and I still had relatives there, Darla had been born and raised in Oklahoma, and we had lived in Tulsa not many years before. I left Washington having accepted the position of Director of Research of the Ada laboratory.

On the plane returning to Wisconsin, I began to ponder what I had done. How would Darla and the children react, what would be the consequences of leaving my job with the University of Wisconsin after only two years, would we like living in Ada, Oklahoma, a much smaller town than our family had ever lived in? I arrived in Madison with much uncertainty and trepidation.

When I broke the news to Darla and the children their reactions were positive. They were wholeheartedly in agreement with the thought of returning to a place they knew well, closer to family and old friends. Although we had enjoyed our time in Madison, we all seemed to be in agreement that the move was the right thing to do. My next hurdle was informing the university that I would be leaving at the end of the school year.

The next day I told Jerry Rollick of my decision. With his close ties to the U.S. Public Health Service, he was aware of the new laboratories. He thought it was great that I had been selected for Director of Research at one of them and gave his blessing. I next made an appointment with the chairman of the department. He politely expressed his feeling of loss for the department but had no objection to my leaving and offered his congratulations. It was agreed that I would finish the semester and leave at the beginning of the summer. So the die was cast—no turning back.

X

My Years in Ada

I had my first big taste of government red tape when we were preparing to move from Madison. As soon as school was out in the spring, we advertised our house for sale, thinking we would have all summer to sell our house and get moved to Oklahoma. To our surprise we had a buyer within the week. They had the cash and said they would have to have possession within a month. So instead of having the summer to sell and move, we had to be out of our house by the end of a month.

As soon as I was sure that the deal would go through, I made arrangements with a moving company and called my contact in the Public Health Service to tell him we were ready to move. He asked me about the moving company, dates, and other information. Everything seemed to be in order, and I was told that I would be sent Government Travel Orders. In talking to Dr. Weinberg we had set no reporting date but had left it open, not knowing how long it would take to sell our home.

In the following days we were busy getting our affairs in order and getting our things ready for the move. The day before our mover was scheduled to load I had still not received Travel Orders, so I called my Public Health Service man. I informed him that we would be loading the next morning, and I hadn't received the Travel Orders. His response was quick and very emphatic: "If you let the movers load your furniture before you have Travel Orders, the government may not pay for the move." I had talked to this person several times since my initial contact, and he had always assured me everything was in order. Upon his announcement that our move might not be paid for, I erupted. Not only would the moving van be there the next morning, we were bumping up against the day we had to give possession to the new owners. In no uncertain terms, and not too civilly, I shouted: "Listen to me, we are loading our furniture in the morning and leaving for Oklahoma and you had better find a way to pay for our move!" Early the next morning, even before the movers had arrived, I received a call from the Public Health Service man telling me that he had worked things out for the move to be paid for even though I would not have the Travel Orders; I would pick up the Travel Orders in Oklahoma. This was my introduction to government red tape.

The move went well, and we settled into a nice house that we had rented on an earlier house-hunting trip. I reported for duty August 31, 1964, and was the third staff member to report to the laboratory. An administrative man, Carl Thompson, had been assigned from the Dallas Regional Office to act as liaison with the community and the contractors. He and his secretary were the only personnel on site when I reported. Dick Vaughn, who would be the Laboratory Director, and Grover Morris, to be Director of Technical Services, had been assigned but would not report until sometime later. The laboratory would have three programs: research, technical services, and training, with a director heading each program.

Ada was a small town of about 15,000 population, the County Seat of Pontotoc County. The economic base was agriculture, mostly cattle ranching. Some very large ranches were located in the area. The Turner Ranch, located just south of town, consisted of thousands of acres. The ranch produced some of the best Hereford cattle in the nation, the number of their blue ribbon winners attesting to the quality of the herd. There were two major industries in town, a cement plant and the Solo Cup Plant. These industries had fairly good payrolls, but the largest employer in town was East Central State College, a four-year liberal arts college.

Ada had some beautiful homes. On the south side of town the street known as Kings Row was lined with very large mansions, some of them were architectural gems. In the 1920s the Fittstown oil field was brought in about ten miles south of Ada, creating much wealth for the area. Many of the newly wealthy built these monstrous homes on Kings Row. Through the years the oil was depleted, but the wealth stayed in Ada. This one isolated area was not typical of residences in Ada; most of the homes were more modest.

Having arrived the end of August, we had only a short time before enrolling the children in school. Darla Ann started in an elementary school fairly close to our home, but Curt, in his first year of Junior High School, had to go across town. Ada did not have public transportation, so their mother or I had to taxi them to school every day. The school system had high standards, and we were very pleased with it. Both of the children would attend the Ada school system through their graduation from High School.

When I arrived in Ada, the laboratory was just a hole in the ground. This was literally true, as the construction contractor had just excavated for the basement. As we watched the laboratory being constructed during the next months, we had temporary offices on the campus of East Central State College. During the next year our primary activity was recruiting staff for the laboratory: chemists, biologists, microbiologists, and engineers were needed. Recruiting professional people for the laboratory was not easy. Ada was a small rural town, with the closest large city, Oklahoma City, almost 100 miles away. Cultural activities and other attractions were few. As word got around of the new laboratory we were surprised with the number of professionals that contacted us who were originally from Oklahoma but had to seek employment elsewhere because of lack of employment opportunities in their home state. Many of our good employees came from these people.

A few weeks after we settled in Ada, Dick Vaughn and his family arrived from Michigan where he had been director of a study of the Great Lakes. Dick and his wife, Laura, had two children about the ages of Curt and Darla Ann. We introduced them around town and helped them get settled in. Shortly thereafter Grover Morris and his wife also arrived.

In addition to our recruiting efforts, we decided that we should get acquainted with our region and let our region know about us. The regions served by the laboratories were based on river basins. Our region included the lower Mississippi River Basin and its tributaries on the east and north, the Colorado River Basin and its tributaries on the west, and the Gulf of Mexico on the south. This area encompassed the states of Louisiana, Arkansas, Oklahoma, Texas, New Mexico, Arizona, and parts of Mississippi, Tennessee, Missouri, Kansas, Colorado, Wyoming, Utah, Nevada, and California. This was an unrealistic area for one laboratory to cover, and later the Colorado River basin was dropped and another laboratory to handle the extreme western area was established in Las Vegas, NV. We decided that our best targets would be state agencies and major universities in the various states. We developed presentations explaining the organization of the laboratory and the mission of the programs, and Dick, Grover, and I took off. In the next months we traveled many miles and made presentations throughout our region.

Congress had passed legislation officially naming the laboratory the Robert S. Kerr Water Research Center. Kerr, who had died in 1963, had been a long-time senator from Oklahoma, and he was one of the most powerful politicians in Washington. Senator Kerr was born near Ada, and the restored log cabin that he was born in, and where he lived as a child, is located on property adjacent to the laboratory. He is buried in a tomb on a knoll overlooking the restored cabin.

He studied at East Central State College (at that time East Central Normal College), became a lawyer, and practiced law in Ada in the early 1920s. In 1926 he became involved in oil drilling, founded the Kerr-McGee Oil Company, and built a large fortune. He was Governor of Oklahoma from 1943 to 1947 and was elected to the U.S. Senate in 1948.

The legislation authorizing the seven laboratories included certain criteria for their locations. One of these criteria was that they should be located near a major research university that could be a resource for the laboratories and which the laboratories could complement. Ada was the home of East Central State College, hardly a major research university. In contrast, the laboratory for the southeastern region was to be located in Athens, Georgia, home of the University of Georgia, and the site of the northwestern region was to be Corvallis, Oregon, home of Oregon State University. During our presentations, an inevitable question was, "Why was the laboratory located in Ada, Oklahoma?" With as straight a face as we could muster, we would seriously answer, "The selection committee looked at all possible sites and concluded that Ada would be the best location." Everyone recognized that the location of the laboratory was due to Senator Kerr's influence.

Shortly after moving to Ada, I saw a notice in the paper that the Ada Community Theater was having auditions for their upcoming play. I had done some acting in a little theater group when we lived in Tulsa, and I was interested. I arrived at Jean Ray's home the evening of the auditions expecting to have to read and compete for a part. Jean was the director of the theater group and also on the faculty of East Central State College. She and the others who were there were surprised to see me. In the past they had put notices in the paper announcing auditions, but seldom did anyone respond. Jean usually had to round up a cast from those in the community whom she knew were interested in acting. I was warmly received and assured that I would be in the cast. The play that was to be done was *Twelve Angry Men*, and I was cast as

Juror Number 7. Our performances were held in an old downtown movie theater that had long since ceased being used for movies. I became a regular with the group, doing several plays in the next few years. The group also did one musical production each summer in the amphitheater at Wintersmith Park. I did several of these including *Finnegan's Rainbow*.

Before the Kerr Center building was completed we had hired a number of people, and our temporary quarters on the college campus were quite crowded. Our Director of Training, Mildred Smith, had also joined us, rounding out the key laboratory staff. Dick, Grover, and Mildred were Public Health Service Officers; Carl and I were Civil Service employees. The other personnel that had come on board were divided between PHS Officers and Civil Service.

The building was finally completed, a beautiful 50,000 square-foot three-story building with basement. The various laboratories had the latest equipment, and the offices were nicely furnished. The director's office was large, carpeted, with private bathroom and elaborately furnished. My office and that of the Director of Technical Services was as large, carpeted, and very well furnished, but without a private bathroom. We had to walk a few steps down the hall to relieve ourselves. The office of the Director of Training was about half the size of our offices and not nearly as elaborately furnished. I guess this gave a clue to the priority of the training program versus the research and technical services programs

We completed our move into the new building in the spring of 1966 and had a dedication program May 28. Dignitaries from Washington, the Dallas Regional office, the State of Oklahoma, and the City of Ada were in attendance. The main speaker for the event was Henry Bellman, Governor of Oklahoma, who later represented Oklahoma in the U.S. Senate. The dedication program was followed by tours of the facility, of which we were all quite proud.

As soon as we settled in Ada we joined the First Baptist Church and the family became very active. I was soon elected to the Board of Deacons, later serving as Chairman. I taught Sunday school classes, sang in the choir, and served on many committees. Darla also taught Sunday school and was active in other church programs. The children attended Sunday school regularly and were active in the youth choirs and other youth programs. The First Baptist was the largest church in town and exerted a lot of influence in the community, as many of the community leaders were members.

As the Kerr Center employees began to arrive in town and began to settle into the activities of the community, they raised many questions in the minds of the Ada residents. After all, Ada was a small rural town, and most of these newcomers were scientists and engineers, professions that were not commonly found in Ada before the arrival of the Kerr Center. Our large building was located on a hill a couple of miles south of town and was easily seen from town. It was a great mystery to most of the residents. In spite of the publicity it had received during its construction and after it had been occupied, most people had little idea of what went on out there. I remember being frequently asked, "How many people work at the lab?" My stock answer was, "About half of them."

I have always loved livestock. I guess this is because my father was a rancher when I was young, and I was around cattle and sheep when I was growing up. I didn't follow in my father's footsteps, but as an adult I always wanted to have a piece of land where I could have a few cattle and maybe a horse or two. My dream finally became reality when we moved to Oklahoma.

Shortly after settling in Ada, I was able to purchase a hundred acres of pastureland. In a short time I acquired a small herd of about 20 beef cattle, which the place could easily support. My mini-ranch was about eight miles west of town; no one lived on the place. I would drive out there after work and on weekends to take care of feeding, pasture mowing, and other chores. I bought two horses, Lady, a thoroughbred and quarter horse mix, and her two-year-old filly. Lady was my favorite; I often rode her when making my rounds. I loved the role of part-time rancher, although I am sure I would have felt differently if I had had to make my living from it. I was what the IRS calls a "hobby farmer."

As the Center became fully staffed, our research program began to take on projects of real significance. Since the research was water-related and was to address the problems of our region, we concentrated on studies of reservoir and stream water quality. One major project related to the problem of deteriorating water quality in reservoirs. This project explored ways of reducing the septic conditions in reservoirs due to seasonal stratification. Another problem in many of the western streams is salinity. We undertook a project in a tributary of the Red River, which had high salinity, to determine ways of controlling the salt deposits. We were all very excited to be involved in meaningful research, and we devoted our full effort to the work.

The Center was originally authorized as a U.S. Public Health Service facility, which was under the Department of Health, Education and Welfare. In the late 1960s a new agency, the Federal Water Pollution Control Administration, was created within the Department of Interior, and the Kerr Center was assigned to it. Since we were no longer under the Public Health Service, all PHS officers at the laboratory had to either convert to Civil Service or be reassigned. Some of them changed to Civil Service, but many stayed in the PHS and were transferred, including our Director, Dick Vaughn, and Grover Morris, Director of Technical Services. Bill Gallagher, Deputy Director of the Dallas Regional Office took over as Kerr Center Director, and Marvin Wood, from the State of Arkansas' environmental program, joined us as Director of Technical Services.

A major change occurred in the organization and mission of the Kerr Center in the late 1960s. The mission of the Center was changed from regional to national. Our laboratory and our sister laboratories were given specific areas of research that would be nationally applicable. The Kerr Center had three areas of research designated: ground water, industrial wastes, and pollution control by means other than conventional treatment. The Center was organized into three branches headed by branch chiefs, reporting to the Kerr Center Director. I became the chief of the Waste Management Branch concerned with pollution control by means other than conventional treatment. The areas that we concentrated in were: agricultural water reuse, control of industrial wastes, and product modification to reduce pollution.

One Saturday morning in January 1970, I was at home when I received a call from Bill Cawley of our Washington office. He told me that I needed to make a trip to Sweden to determine what the Swedes were doing about phosphates in detergents. One of the hot topics at that time was eutrophication of lakes and reservoirs, which was blamed largely on the phosphates in laundry detergents. Our Washington people had received word that the Swedes had developed detergents that contained no phosphates, and they were interested in learning about it. Since one of the areas of research of my branch was product modification to reduce pollution, I was one of those who should go. I had only about three weeks before the trip, and I didn't have an official passport. This could be a problem. I immediately got a passport application and sent it in. Based on what I had heard, I had little hope that I would receive the passport in time for the trip. It was a really close call: the passport was hand-delivered to me at my home the afternoon before I was to leave the following day. The only reason I received such service was that I was a good friend of the Ada postmaster and he was watching out for the passport.

I was one of a team of three that traveled to Sweden. Of the other two, one was from our Cincinnati laboratory, the other was from Washington Headquarters. I flew from Oklahoma City to Chicago where I met my Cincinnati counterpart. We would meet the Washington representative in Sweden. We had a long flight from Chicago to Stockholm with a stop in Stavanger, Norway, arriving in Stockholm the morning of the following day. We were met by a delegation of government officials and escorted to our hotel. Depositing us in our hotel, they announced that our first meeting would be at two o'clock that afternoon. After such a long flight, all we wanted was sleep, but we complied nevertheless, not wanting to cause an international incident. I doubt that we contributed much to the first meeting.

The next two days were spent in conferences with Swedish government officials and industry and scientific representatives. A delegation from Canada also joined us because of the U.S.-Canadian Joint Commission on water quality of the Great Lakes. The third day we traveled to Uppsala, a short train ride, to visit the university. There we conferred with professors who were engaged in research on the phosphate problem. We returned to Stockholm that evening. Our fourth and final day was spent in meetings to summarize what had been discussed the previous days.

Stockholm, in the middle of winter, was truly a fairyland with everything covered in snow. The city looked like a Currier and Ives picture. At that time of year, as close to the Artic Circle as we were, the days were very short. The sun was not seen until ten or eleven o'clock in the morning, and it would start getting dark by about three o'clock in the afternoon. Consequently, the streetlights were on most of the time, which added to the awe.

On our return to the states, we prepared a report of our trip. We had found that Sweden had not completely solved the phosphate problem, as we had been led to believe, but they did have some low-level products on the market. These products were not being well-received, however, having gained only about 20 per cent of the market. Swedish appliance makers and housewives were averse to change, as most of us are. We accelerated our research in this area in two directions: removing the phosphates from detergents, and developing treatment processes to remove the phosphates from discharged waters.

My trip to Sweden was the first of several official overseas trips in the next few years.

In December 1970, the Environmental Protection Agency was created. This new agency brought together various environmental-related programs that were previously scattered within several governmental agencies. Included were the water pollution programs of the Interior Department, which included the Kerr Research Center. During the short life of the Kerr Center it had been reorganized and reassigned several times, but now it had a new home within an agency which promised to have more influence and standing than previous homes. Most of us felt that the change was a good one.

In the mid-1970s Bud Womsley and his family moved to Ada. They joined the First Baptist Church and we became good friends. He was a salesman and did a lot of traveling, but in the past he had been a musician—I think at one time he traveled with a circus band. He learned that I played trombone, although I had not played in several years, and he wanted to organize a band. He recruited several other musicians, including my friend Jack Keeley from the Kerr Center, and we started practicing. I remember that we had two trumpets, trombone, clarinet, drums, and tuba played by Jack—there may have been others from time to time. Womsley owned an old fire engine so we called the band The Fireman's Half-fast Marching Band, and we rode on the fire engine in parades and when we went to places to play. We played mostly Dixieland and had a lot of fun. The band disbanded in a couple of years when Womsley moved from

Ada. The tuba that Jack played belonged to Womsley, and the last time I heard from Jack it was still in Jack's attic. This was the last time I played in a band.

By the mid-1970s a major research area of my branch was water reuse. Because of the high priority given this subject, I made an inspection trip to Australia in October of 1974. For many years, several locations in Australia had successfully practiced agricultural reuse of water. One need in the EPA programs was for good reliable data for designing reuse systems. By visiting Australia it was felt that we could collect the most reliable data in a short time for the least cost. Belford Seabrook, of one of EPA's headquarters operating programs, accompanied me. After our initial visit to the Warribee Farm, operated by the Melbourne and Metropolitan Board of Works, Seabrook and I went separate ways in order to cover the most territory. The official part of my trip included visits to Melbourne, Traralgon, and Mildura in Victoria; Broken Hill in New South Wales; and Adalaide in South Australia. Darla accompanied me on this trip—in those days there were few restrictions on extra time attached to foreign trips. Following my official visits, we spent time in Sidney, and on our return trip we had stopovers in New Zealand and Tahiti.

In September 1976, I received a call from the New York Regional Office requesting someone go to Puerto Rico to assist a rum company with the problem of disposing of their distillery waste. I flew to San Juan where I conferred with the EPA representative on the problem. The next day we traveled by car to Ponce, on the south coast of the island, where I was introduced to officials of the Barcardi Rum Company. I spent two days going over their system and making recommendations. The next few days, before going home, I drove around the island enjoying the scenery and discovering the diversity of such a small piece of land.

When World War II ended, my father resigned his position at Consolidated Aircraft, and started working as a buyer at the

Fort Worth Stockyards. Once again he was doing what he enjoyed the most: working with livestock. Also, he was his own boss. Except for the years during the depression, when he worked for the Highway Department and Neeley's Grocery Store in Kerrville, and during the war when he worked at Consolidated, he had always been his own boss. He bought cattle, sheep, and hogs for people who placed orders with him and sometime he would buy cattle for his own account.

A few years later my parents bought a small farm near Alvarado, Texas, about 20 miles south of Fort Worth. They continued to live in Fort Worth while my father built a new house on the place. My father was a very good carpenter and did all of the work in building the house, including a beautiful stone fireplace. Working alone, it took quite a long time to complete the house, but in time it was completed and they moved into their new home.

Daddy had cattle on the farm and he also had hogs. He was back in his orbit with the livestock. They lived only two or three miles from Alvarado which was convenient for shopping. They became very active in the Alvarado Baptist Church and had lots of friends.

In time the farm became too much for them to handle. They sold the farm and bought a house in Alvarado. The house was on a large corner lot and so they had room for a garden. Daddy missed having livestock to work with, so he bought a small tract of land (10 acres I think) which was adjacent to town and where he could have a few head of cattle. The place needed fencing so Daddy acquired used railroad ties to use as fence posts. Building the fence was hard work. The railroad ties were very heavy, certainly too heavy for a man in his 80s to handle by himself. Nevertheless, he was determined to finish the job.

One day during the time he was building the fence, he had a fainting spell when he was in town. He was rushed to the hospital in Cleburne, about 10 miles from Alvarado, the closest hospital. In a couple of days he was released from the hospital, all the tests being negative.

A few days after returning home, he returned to his fencing project, contrary to his doctor's advice to take it easy. The second day after returning to the fencing job, he fell ill and was again rushed to the hospital. This time it was determined that he had had a massive heart attack. He was in the hospital about three days when he died peacefully, November 9, 1976, at 84 years of age. He was buried in the Alvarado Cemetery.

Starting in the 1970s the Environmental Protection Agency sponsored many research projects in foreign countries using what we called "P.L. 480" money. P.L. 480 was a common name for the Agricultural Trade Development and Assistance Act of 1954, which established food aid programs for developing countries. I have no idea how this all worked, but under this program the United States accumulated funds in countries where the funds could not be taken out of the country but could be used by the United States within the host country. With these funds, EPA sponsored research projects in India, Egypt, Poland, and other countries. I became the project officer for a P.L. 480 project in Poland conducted by the Research Institute in Wroclaw.

In September of 1978 I made a trip to Poland to review my project, and Darla went with me. We flew on Pan American Airways to Vienna, Austria, where we had to change to the Polish Airline LOT. Poland was still behind the "Iron Curtain" at that time, and few if any airlines from the western countries could fly into Poland. We spent two days in Vienna before continuing to Poland.

Before we left home we had hoped to visit some other countries in Eastern Europe but had not made any arrangements. During our stopover in Vienna, I learned that the embassies of Hungry and Yugoslavia were just around the corner from our hotel. The second morning we were there, I walked to these embassies to see what I could learn. I first went to the Hungarian embassy and inquired about visas to visit their country. To my surprise, all I had to do was fill out a short application and pay a small fee—probably equilivant to about $10 US—and I had our visas. I next went to the Yugoslavian embassy and was again surprised at the ease with which I was able to get visas. I was later told that if I had applied for visas while still in Oklahoma, it would have probably taken an inordinate amount of time to get them.

We flew into Warsaw and changed to a flight to Wroclaw where people from the research institute met us. Fortunately, most of them spoke good English—certainly better English than I spoke Polish. We were put up in a nice hotel and during our entire stay were treated like royalty. I was impressed by their work on the research project; they were very receptive to any suggestion or comment I made. I had heard so many stories that the P.L. 480 projects were a waste of time, but I was very pleased with my project.

When we arrived in Wroclaw, I had no luggage. Darla's luggage arrived, but I had no checked bags. It was very difficult to communicate with the airline personnel, trying to describe my bags. The project people helped, but I finally left the airport sans luggage, being assured it would arrive on the next day's flight. Every day we checked with the airline. A lady in our Warsaw embassy took it on as her project and made multiple calls every day, to no avail. Of course, all the clothes I had were what I was wearing when I arrived in Wroclaw. After two days, the Pan Am people told me to purchase what I needed and the airline would reimburse me when I returned home. One of the men from the Research Institute accompanied me to the local department store for shopping. There was not much to choose from; their sizes made no sense to me. I finally picked out enough "Polish" attire to get me through the week, although the colors were drab and not very stylish by our standards.

After our week in Wroclaw, we returned to Warsaw; by this time I had completely given up on ever seeing my luggage.

We spent the night in Warsaw, and the next afternoon we were leaving the hotel for the airport to take our flight to Hungary. We had checked out of the hotel and were going down the stairs to the lobby when I heard my name being paged over the public address system. I checked the front desk and was told that my luggage was at the airport. We hurried outside, hailed a taxi, and were off to the airport. By the time we reached the airport, we didn't have much time left before our flight was to depart. We ran to the baggage area but could not make anyone understand that I was looking for lost luggage. I was able to maneuver around to where I could see a pile of luggage in a gated enclosure, and there I spied my bags. After what seemed like ages I finally made an attendant understand that my bags were there; he retrieved them and verified the tag on them matched the stubs I had. With only minutes left, we boarded the plane, luggage and all, for Budapest. To this day, I believe that my bags were in the Warsaw airport the entire time we were in Poland.

We had decided that our first adventure would be in Hungary; beyond that we had no itinerary for the time following our departure from Poland. Our only firm date was September 27 when we had to be in Amsterdam for our return flight to the states. Our direct flight from Warsaw to Budapest was a little over two hours. On landing at the Budapest airport, or any airport in eastern European countries, the first thing a westerner noticed was the numerous heavily armed soldiers. They were not only at airports, but were common figures throughout major cities. This was true of all the eastern European countries during those years; after all, they were still behind the "Iron Curtain."

At the information counter we were able to change money and get a hotel recommendation. Our taxi ride into the city revealed a city of beautiful buildings lining the banks of the Danube River, although most of them showed signs of neglect. Our hotel was clean and comfortable and well located, but signs of austerity were apparent.

During the next three days we explored the city. We learned that the city of Budapest was created by combining the city of Buda on the right bank of the Danube with the city of Pest on the left bank—or is it the other way around, I can never keep this straight. The parliament building on the bank of the Danube was spectacular as was the Royal Castle. St. Stephens Basilica stood in all its glory in the center of it all. Good restaurants were few so we ate most of our meals either in our hotel room or in a park from food we could purchase from the markets. Our days in Budapest were a wonderful experience, but we had to move on.

Since we were not traveling on an itinerary, we had bought only one-way tickets. Our next destination was Yugoslavia, but where in Yugoslavia? After consulting maps, looking at brochures, and getting what information we could from the information center, we decided our destination would be Dubrovnik, an old medieval city on the Adriatic coast. I don't think the plane we took from Budapest to Dubrovnik would have met our FAA standards. The only good thing about the flight was that it was short.

On arriving in Dubrovnik, we checked at the information center and decided on a hotel in the Old Town. Our hotel was situated over shops that were on the street level, and from our window we looked out over a busy, narrow, cobblestone street. The neighborhood looked like it had not been changed since its development in medieval times.

The main attraction in Old Town was the old fort, which hung on the rocky Adriatic shore. It was completely open to the public to explore at will. We spent hours climbing its walls and turrets. One day we took a tour of the surrounding area. Our guide spoke little English, but with the aid of an English guidebook we were able to make out most of the sights. We saw many medieval castles, stone bridges, farms, and lots of vineyards. Our three days in Dubrovnik were outstanding.

The adventurous spirits we were, we decided to take a bus to our next destination, which was Venice, Italy. This was one of the most interesting experiences of our trip. The bus was the regular bus that traveled that route, no luxury whatsoever. The road, which was narrow and not very well maintained, paralleled the Adriatic coastline. The bus stopped at every town, no matter how small, and the people who got on and off were the ordinary working people of the area. We left Dubrovnik in the middle of the afternoon, and the trip turned out to be an overnight trip.

We arrived in Venice early in the morning. All bus and train terminals were outside the city, so we took a water taxi into Venice proper. Venice is one of the most remarkable cities in the world. (That may be stretching it a bit since I have not visited all the cities in the world.) Even those that have not visited Venice know that their streets are canals. The walkways between the buildings and the canals are usually very narrow. St. Marks Square, inhabited almost exclusively by pigeons, is surrounded by shops and sidewalk cafes on three sides and the Doge's Palace on the other side. The St. Marks Basilica sits to one side and the Bell Tower soars over the Piazza. We spent two days in Venice, which was time well-spent.

From Venice we traveled by train to Florence and then on to Milan, spending two full days in each city. In Milan we boarded a train and said good-by to Italy: our destination was Cologne, Germany. I wanted to visit the Cologne Cathedral. In route to Cologne we stopped for a day in Heidelberg. I had spent six months in Heidelberg in our army of occupation at the end of World War II. I was not disappointed in seeing the Cologne Cathedral. It is a magnificent building.

Following Cologne we pressed on to our final European destination, Amsterdam. We arrived there in time to spend a

one is free to interpret the Bible for him or her s
terpretation had better conform to accepted Bapt
etation. While one is encouraged to seek God's wi
s seem to have advance notice what that will shoul
he message you receive from the Divine is different
u are either not hearing God correctly or you are no
honest.

I would have continued going through the motions of
d" Baptist, while growing more spiritually isolated
y mainstream fellow church members, except for my
problems which ended in divorce.

nd I had married during World War II. Many, like us,
that marrying was the thing to do before the "boys
d off to war." This was the theme of so many motion
s of that day, and many of us were caught up in the
f the times. We agreed not to have children while I
the Army, and following my discharge I returned to
for the next four years, and during that time we
want children. We were married about eight years
Curt was born.

he time Curt and Darla Ann were grown and gone
ome, Darla and I were occupied with common
s, which formed a basis for a relationship. Once the
n were reared and away from home there was little
ind us together, and our marriage deteriorated as we
rther and further apart. Our relationship reached the
g point in April 1980, and I moved out and rented an
nt. Our divorce was granted January 28, 1981. I will
nto the details but will say that it was very difficult
amily, and I acknowledge my share of the blame.

n as word spread around town that the Harlins were
marital problems—and it doesn't take long in a town
of Ada, Oklahoma—I felt a drastic change in my
ce by the members of the First Baptist Church.
h I had been a faithful member for more than 16
ad sung in the choir, taught Sunday school classes,

couple of days sightseeing before our departure for home. We had spent four weeks in Europe, traveled hundreds of miles and had a wonderful time.

I had hardly returned from my trip to Poland when, in October 1978, it was my privilege to return to Australia. This time I was invited to be the keynote speaker at an international conference on water reuse, which was held in Melbourne. After the conference, and before leaving Australia, I met with groups in Sidney and Brisbane to present information on our research activities at the Kerr Center that were of mutual interest. On my return trip I spent a few relaxing days in Fiji. I learned, to my surprise, that in Fiji vehicles traveled on the left side of the road. This was no problem as I had driven the previous two weeks on the left side of the roads in Australia.

Curt was always an energetic boy. As soon as he was old enough, he got a job delivering the local morning newspaper. He was very conscientious about getting up early—about four o'clock in the morning—without any prodding from his parents. He made his deliveries on his bicycle, except on rainy days when I would make his rounds with him in the car. As soon as he reached his 14th birthday, he started agitating to get a Honda cycle. In those days the Honda cycle was the status symbol of teenagers. I resisted, because I felt they were too dangerous for drivers of that age. In fact, several of Curt's friends had had serious accidents with them. This didn't deter him though. According to him, he was the only 14-year-old in town who didn't have a Honda.

After several days of listening to his appeal, I said, "Curt, I'm not going to buy you a Honda, but if you save enough money to buy one, I won't keep you from buying it." This was a mistake: Curt became a miser. He saved every nickel he made and would not spend any money that was not absolutely necessary. Before very long he had enough money and had his Honda. Fortunately he never had any serious accidents.

As soon as he was 16, he got a job bagging groceries at the local supermarket, which was better hours, and more money.

In the spring of 1980 I was invited by the World Health Organization to participate in a conference on water reuse in arid countries that was to be held in Algiers. The World Health Organization was to pay for my trip. I thought this was a good deal, but I soon found out that it was not as easy as I assumed it would be. I discovered that our government would not allow a third party to pay an employees' travel expenses while he or she was on the government's payroll. I had to take annual leave and go as a WHO consultant. During this time there was much turmoil in Africa and the Middle East, and I learned that the State Department had Algeria on the dangerous list and recommended only essential travel to that country. After conversations with EPA's travel office and much soul-searching, I decided to make the trip. The trip went well and I returned home safely.

I presented two papers at the conference. This was my first and only experience in giving a paper to a multilingual audience and having to observe the timing of the translators. It was quite an experience, and I made several contacts that I benefited from in the following years.

During the years in Ada we made many friends. The time was enjoyable for the family, although the years were very busy for me, at times hectic, in my job. Curt graduated from high school in 1969, and Darla Ann graduated in 1971. They both enrolled in East Central State College. Curt transferred to the University of Oklahoma after his sophomore year and obtained a degree in pharmacy. Darla Ann was majoring in music but dropped out of college in her junior year after getting married.

Our years in Ada were good years for the family and very rewarding for me professionally. What lay ahead was a shock to our friends and heart wrenching for the family.

XI

From Ada to Washi

During our years in Ada the fam community very well. Darla and I and community activities; we made man and Curt did well in school; Darla Ann and other musical programs, and Curt They both were married in the early 197(

I was very busy in my job, and in the l; traveling, requiring me to be away fro saw more of our world and was expo ideas and beliefs, I became more aware life were not always black or white. Th thought about the profound issues of Go purpose of life, the more gray issues I en

As my concern with these issues intens uncertain about my place in the B teachings are fundamental to all Baptis the exclusive guide of faith and pract priesthood of believers, meaning that access to God—no priest, bishop, Po church, needed as intermediary. The teaching is that we all are capable and on-one, with God in working out our sa

I have no problem with either of these teachings contained in the Bible are t lives, and we can approach God and be open to Him. So I accept these two fur Baptists. But teachings and practice c;

couple of days sightseeing before our departure for home. We had spent four weeks in Europe, traveled hundreds of miles and had a wonderful time.

I had hardly returned from my trip to Poland when, in October 1978, it was my privilege to return to Australia. This time I was invited to be the keynote speaker at an international conference on water reuse, which was held in Melbourne. After the conference, and before leaving Australia, I met with groups in Sidney and Brisbane to present information on our research activities at the Kerr Center that were of mutual interest. On my return trip I spent a few relaxing days in Fiji. I learned, to my surprise, that in Fiji vehicles traveled on the left side of the road. This was no problem as I had driven the previous two weeks on the left side of the roads in Australia.

Curt was always an energetic boy. As soon as he was old enough, he got a job delivering the local morning newspaper. He was very conscientious about getting up early—about four o'clock in the morning—without any prodding from his parents. He made his deliveries on his bicycle, except on rainy days when I would make his rounds with him in the car. As soon as he reached his 14th birthday, he started agitating to get a Honda cycle. In those days the Honda cycle was the status symbol of teenagers. I resisted, because I felt they were too dangerous for drivers of that age. In fact, several of Curt's friends had had serious accidents with them. This didn't deter him though. According to him, he was the only 14-year-old in town who didn't have a Honda.

After several days of listening to his appeal, I said, "Curt, I'm not going to buy you a Honda, but if you save enough money to buy one, I won't keep you from buying it." This was a mistake: Curt became a miser. He saved every nickel he made and would not spend any money that was not absolutely necessary. Before very long he had enough money and had his Honda. Fortunately he never had any serious accidents.

As soon as he was 16, he got a job bagging groceries at the local supermarket, which was better hours, and more money.

In the spring of 1980 I was invited by the World Health Organization to participate in a conference on water reuse in arid countries that was to be held in Algiers. The World Health Organization was to pay for my trip. I thought this was a good deal, but I soon found out that it was not as easy as I assumed it would be. I discovered that our government would not allow a third party to pay an employees' travel expenses while he or she was on the government's payroll. I had to take annual leave and go as a WHO consultant. During this time there was much turmoil in Africa and the Middle East, and I learned that the State Department had Algeria on the dangerous list and recommended only essential travel to that country. After conversations with EPA's travel office and much soul-searching, I decided to make the trip. The trip went well and I returned home safely.

I presented two papers at the conference. This was my first and only experience in giving a paper to a multilingual audience and having to observe the timing of the translators. It was quite an experience, and I made several contacts that I benefited from in the following years.

During the years in Ada we made many friends. The time was enjoyable for the family, although the years were very busy for me, at times hectic, in my job. Curt graduated from high school in 1969, and Darla Ann graduated in 1971. They both enrolled in East Central State College. Curt transferred to the University of Oklahoma after his sophomore year and obtained a degree in pharmacy. Darla Ann was majoring in music but dropped out of college in her junior year after getting married.

Our years in Ada were good years for the family and very rewarding for me professionally. What lay ahead was a shock to our friends and heart wrenching for the family.

XI

From Ada to Washington

During our years in Ada the family settled into the community very well. Darla and I were busy in church and community activities; we made many friends. Darla Ann and Curt did well in school; Darla Ann participated in choral and other musical programs, and Curt played in the band. They both were married in the early 1970s.

I was very busy in my job, and in the latter years did much traveling, requiring me to be away from home often. As I saw more of our world and was exposed to more diverse ideas and beliefs, I became more aware that major issues of life were not always black or white. The more I studied and thought about the profound issues of God, humanity, and the purpose of life, the more gray issues I encountered.

As my concern with these issues intensified, I became more uncertain about my place in the Baptist Church. Two teachings are fundamental to all Baptists: first, the Bible is the exclusive guide of faith and practice; and second, the priesthood of believers, meaning that all of us have direct access to God—no priest, bishop, Pope, committee, even church, needed as intermediary. The consequence of this teaching is that we all are capable and required to deal, one-on-one, with God in working out our salvation.

I have no problem with either of these teaching. I believe the teachings contained in the Bible are the best guide for our lives, and we can approach God and be led by Him if we are open to Him. So I accept these two fundamental teachings of Baptists. But teachings and practice can be different things.

While one is free to interpret the Bible for him or her self that interpretation had better conform to accepted Baptist interpretation. While one is encouraged to seek God's will, Baptists seem to have advance notice what that will should be. If the message you receive from the Divine is different, then you are either not hearing God correctly or you are not being honest.

I guess I would have continued going through the motions of a "good" Baptist, while growing more spiritually isolated from my mainstream fellow church members, except for my marital problems which ended in divorce.

Darla and I had married during World War II. Many, like us, thought that marrying was the thing to do before the "boys marched off to war." This was the theme of so many motion pictures of that day, and many of us were caught up in the spell of the times. We agreed not to have children while I was in the Army, and following my discharge I returned to college for the next four years, and during that time we didn't want children. We were married about eight years before Curt was born.

Until the time Curt and Darla Ann were grown and gone from home, Darla and I were occupied with common interests, which formed a basis for a relationship. Once the children were reared and away from home there was little left to bind us together, and our marriage deteriorated as we grew further and further apart. Our relationship reached the breaking point in April 1980, and I moved out and rented an apartment. Our divorce was granted January 28, 1981. I will not go into the details but will say that it was very difficult for the family, and I acknowledge my share of the blame.

As soon as word spread around town that the Harlins were having marital problems—and it doesn't take long in a town the size of Ada, Oklahoma—I felt a drastic change in my acceptance by the members of the First Baptist Church. Although I had been a faithful member for more than 16 years, had sung in the choir, taught Sunday school classes, served on various committees, and had even been chairman of the Deacons, overnight I was a stranger. No, I was not treated as a stranger; Baptists pride themselves on making the stranger and visitor feel welcome. I was treated like one with an incurable communicable disease whom should be avoided at all cost.

I could no longer worship in an environment that I felt totally unwelcome in, so I tried other churches. After awhile, I began going regularly to a Presbyterian Church. I already had friends there; in fact the pastor and I were in the Rotary Club together. I felt welcomed in that church. Once again I felt good about attending church, although I didn't join the Presbyterian Church.

As time passed, I sensed that people at work felt uncomfortable with me—they didn't seem to know how to deal with me. Many of my colleagues and their wives had been good friends of Darla's and mine, and we had socialized regularly with many of them. Some tried to maintain their neutrality, some continued as cordial as ever, and a few were outright hostile. I soon concluded that I needed to leave Ada and started actively looking for transfer opportunities. I sent out several applications to other EPA components, but it was soon apparent that there were few opportunities for a person of my grade, and I didn't want to take a reduction in grade.

At that time I had a big research project in Lubbock, Texas. In the beginning I had tried to handle it from the laboratory, but it soon became apparent that I needed an on-site manager. We were able to get a man from headquarters, George Keeler, who wanted to leave the Washington area, assigned to the project to be the on-site manager. He had been in Lubbock over a year at the time I was looking for a transfer, and at that time he was being pressured to return to Washington, which he didn't want to do. The solution to both of our situations was evident: George move to Ada and take my job and I transfer to Washington to fill his position. Everyone concerned agreed, and it was settled.

The date for my transfer from the Kerr Center to Washington was August 1, 1981. I had a few household items and furniture that I had to move. It wasn't much but was more than I could transport in my car. In our divorce settlement I took only a few items that were exclusively mine or were of sentimental value. Darla retained our home and the furnishing, while I was given the farm. The movers loaded my belongings the morning of August the first and I left by car the middle of the afternoon, my car loaded with clothes and small items.

I picked up I-40 east of Oklahoma City and was in Arkansas by nightfall. Continuing on across Arkansas on I-40, I crossed the Mississippi River and entered Tennessee at Memphis. The drive the entire length of Tennessee was through some of the most scenic country on earth. I left I-40 for I-81 a few miles east of Knoxville, and I was soon in Virginia. The drive through western Virginia is every bit as spectacular as Tennessee. The ever-changing Blue Ridge Mountains are natural beauty beyond compare. I arrived in Arlington, Virginia, about noon on the third day after leaving Ada and checked into a Holiday Inn. I didn't want to live in D.C. and Arlington was convenient and safer. I had often stayed in Arlington on my many trips to Washington, so I was somewhat familiar with the area. Now I had to settle down to a new life.

The next morning I called Bill Rosenkranz, who would be my new boss, to announce my arrival. He told me to take as much time as I needed to find a place to live and get settled.

After looking at several apartments, I settled on an efficiency apartment in Arlington that was small but nice. My financial means, reduced considerably by the alimony I was required to pay monthly, limited what I could afford. It was OK though, all I really needed was a place to sleep and eat. The apartment was on the ground floor in a nice high-rise apartment building and only a short walk to the Metro stop. It had been one of the first high-rise apartment buildings in the area, and in its early days, I was told, was a show place in Arlington. Through the years it had retained its elegance and was one of the few buildings that still had a uniformed doorman. It was unfurnished so my next task was to buy some furniture.

The apartment consisted of one large room to be used as living room, bedroom, and dining room; a small kitchen; an alcove, which I used for a reading and television room; and bath. In a few days I had acquired, during visits to flea markets and Woodies Warehouse, the essentials for "light housekeeping." I had a nice couch that could be made into a bed, a nice table with chairs for eating and miscellaneous uses, a couple of living room chairs, and lamps to complete the decor. I had brought my favorite lounge chair and television from Oklahoma. It wasn't very long before I checked out of the Holiday Inn and settled in my new quarters.

My new assignment was Chief of the Drinking Water Research program. In this position I was responsible for preparing the annual research plan and budget for drinking water research that was conducted in several of the EPA research laboratories. During the year I was responsible for monitoring the research to ensure that it was carried out according to the plan and within the budget. Most of the research was conducted in the Cincinnati laboratory, with minor amounts in the Corvallis and Athens laboratories. I knew the researchers in the various laboratories through contacts over the past years, so I had a good relationship with all of them.

Not long after I settled in Arlington, I joined a carpool with three other EPA employees who lived near me. Three of us took weekly turns driving; the young lady who rode with us didn't have a car, so she paid a few dollars for her ride. This was a new experience for me, although a common practice in cities. Driving in the Washington area was nothing like driving in Ada. In Ada rush hour traffic was defined as having to wait for two cars at an intersection. It was different in Washington.

I settled into my job fairly easily, although it was quite different than my job in Ada. One big difference was that everything that was done had to be done in a great hurry and with a lot of anxiety. It seemed that the bosses would deliberately wait till the last minute to need something, so it would be a big crisis. Even routine things somehow always became hectic. In Ada I had only one boss over me; in Washington I had a multilevel of bosses, and they usually were totally unaware of what the other ones were doing. This made for some interesting situations—really hilarious situations sometimes. I soon learned how the system worked and got along fine. One major difference was that I had no employees to directly supervise. I liked this, although I never really had any difficult employees in Ada.

My work occupied the weekdays, but the weekends gave me opportunities to see the sights of Washington. I had been in Washington many times on business but had never had time to really see all the interesting things that were there—the museums, monuments, parks, the great buildings. During the first few months I took advantage of my Saturdays and Sundays to visit these magnificent places. Some of the places I had visited in the 1960s when the family visited Washington on our big trip, but that had been a long time ago. Now everything seemed new to me.

I made frequent trips to the laboratories that were doing the drinking water research, but the traveling was not nearly as heavy as it had been when I was in Ada. Many of the trips were only overnight; some just for the day. They tended to break the routine that seemed to become burdensome so easily.

After my father died, my mother could not live alone. My sister, Hazel, and I, with my mother's agreement, decided that Mother would divide her time between me and Hazel. We sold her house in Alvarado and we moved her in with

Darla and me in our home in Ada. This was to be for six months, after which she would spend the next six months with Hazel. My mother had her own room, and this arrangement worked well in the beginning. As time passed, we began to notice that Mother's memory was failing, and she developed other health problems.

In time Mother's condition deteriorated until Darla and I could not take proper care of her in our home, so we arranged for her to enter a nursing home in Ada. I made all of the arrangements with the nursing home before telling Mother. One of the hardest things I ever had to do was tell her that we were moving her to the nursing home. With much anxiety I began to explain to Mother that she was going to live in a nursing home, not knowing what her reaction would be. She listened intently as I explained. When I finished she said, "Well C.C. I guess that is the best thing to do." Tears welled up in my eyes and I cried with relief.

I visited Mother in the nursing home every day that I was in town. I did a lot of traveling on my job though, but Darla would visit her when I was out of town. As time passed, Mother didn't know who I was, she just recognized me as someone who visited her often. She was living in the past; she would talk about things she and my father had done years before. It was very sad to see her in this state, but she got along well with the nursing home staff and other patients.

Following my devorce from Darla, I could not see to Mother's needs properly, with my traveling so much, and I could not expect Darla to take care of her. The only thing to do was to move her to Kerrville to be with my sister Hazel. Hazel made arrangements for her to enter a nursing home in Kerrville, and I took her there. Hazel visited her daily, as I had done, and she seemed satisfied in her new home.

A short time after my transfer to Washington, DC, I received a call from Hazel telling me that Mother had passed away. She had gone to bed the night before, as usual, and she never woke up. She died peacefully in her sleep, September 22,

1981, just six days before her 86th birthday. She was buried beside my Father in the Alvarado Cemetery.

As soon as I was settled in Arlington, I began to think about a church. There was a Baptist Church just a few blocks from my apartment, so I decided to try it. After attending it a few times I decided that whether in Ada, Oklahoma, Abilene, Texas, or Arlington, Virginia, Baptist Churches were all the same. I don't say this to my credit, but I had become biased against Baptist Churches.

Through the years, I had done a lot of reading about the Catholic Church and had attended Catholic Churches many times, so I decided to give the Catholics a try. I attended several different Catholic Churches in the Arlington area. Although the liturgy was quite different than what I was used to, I felt very good about the church. One thing that annoyed me about Baptist Churches was the lack of reverence in the services. The talking and visiting among members seemed totally out of place and had bothered me for years. I liked the quiet reverence of the people as they enter the Catholic Church. Rather than starting a conversation with a neighbor, they kneel in prayer or meditation.

I finally settled on St. Charles Church in Arlington and started going there regularly. Father Horace "Tuck" Grinell, the Associate Pastor, was a young, rather unorthodox priest whom I liked from our first meeting. Although I had not met him before, I had heard of him through mutual friends.

Not long after I started attending St. Charles Church, I signed up for an instruction class for adults. Father Tuck taught the class, which lasted several weeks and was very comprehensive. While the liturgy and other practices of the church were very different from what I had grown up with, some of the fundamental beliefs were surprisingly close to those I had brought from the Baptist Church.

Two basic teachings of the Catholic Church, which are far from agreement with Baptist beliefs, concern baptism and

Holy Communion— the Lord's Supper as the Baptists call it. Baptists teach that baptism is simply a saved person's initiation into Church membership and has no saving power. In the Baptist Church baptism follows the conversion experience and therefore Baptists hold that it is not essential to salvation. It is done because of the example of Jesus' baptism. The Catholic teaching, on the other hand, is that at baptism we are freed from original sin and given God's grace-presence. In other words, for Catholics baptism is necessary for salvation.

I must say that for years I had been troubled by the role of baptism in the salvation process. My church, the Baptist, was inflexible in its teaching that baptism played no role in a person's salvation. But as I read the Bible I saw so many references where Jesus, and the apostles, connected baptism with salvation.

Jesus commanded his apostles to, "Go, therefore, and make disciples of all Nations; baptize them in the name of the Father and of the Son and of the Holy Spirit..." Matthew 28:19. Also in Mark 16:16 Jesus said, "He who believes and is baptized will be saved...." Peter replied to the Jews when asked what they must do to be saved, "You must repent...and every one of you must be baptized...," Acts 2:38. I have felt for a long time that there had to be more to baptism than just doing it as an observance of Jesus' example. However, I am not ready to accept that you must be baptized to be saved.

There is also a great gulf between Baptist and Catholic teachings concerning the Lord's Supper. Baptists hold that the Lord's Supper is nothing more than a memorial to our Lord. When Jesus said, "...do this as a memorial to me," in Luke 22:19, that is all there was to it. Baptists are not even consistent in when and how often they observe the Lord's Supper. Probably the most common practice in Baptist Churches is to observe the Lord's Supper ever quarter, or four times a year. Some Baptist Churches may observe it monthly, while some others observe it less often than once a quarter. To a great extent, it seems that the frequency depends on the pastor's preference.

The Catholic Church is quite different. Observance of Holy Communion (the Lord's Supper) is central to every worship service (Mass). It would be impossible to have a Mass without Holy Communion. Catholics believe that the body and blood of Christ is truly present in the bread and wine of the Eucharist (known as transubstantiation). In taking the bread and wine of the Mass, Catholics believe that Christ is actually received into their bodies.

Many other teachings and practices were foreign to me, but most of them simply required getting used to and presented no major shift in what I consider basic beliefs. If I were called on to describe, very simply, the practical difference I found in the two churches, it would be that the Baptist Church requires its members to be morally and spiritually perfect, and since none of us is capable of this they carry around guilt burdens to their detriment. The Catholic Church recognizes our human weaknesses and inability to live perfect lives in this imperfect world and provides the means to return to God to try again.

After weeks of study and preparation, I came into the Catholic Church on Easter eve night, April 10, 1982. At first I would worry about doing the mechanical things correctly and miss the blessings that should have come from the Mass. When to cross myself, where and how to genuflect, when to stand, when to kneel, when to sit were some of the mechanical things that I worried about. In a Baptist Church all you have to do is stand for the opening and closing songs and prayers and in between just sit and listen, sleep, daydream, or any other worthwhile pursuit such as counting the number of ladies who wore hats that day. The Catholic Church is different. You have to be on your toes or you will miss an important cue. Of course, after awhile most of this becomes natural and, I am sorry to say, even mechanical.

One thing I brought from the Baptist Church is my knowledge of the Bible. Going to Sunday school regularly and other Bible study activities in the Baptist Church gave me a good knowledge of the scriptures. This is not true in the Catholic Church. Most Catholics have a very limited knowledge of the Bible. This goes back to the years when they were actually discouraged from Bible-reading. This is changing however, and opportunities for Bible study are now given in most Catholic Churches.

In November 1982 I received one of the greatest shocks of my life. I was talking to my good friend Jack Keeley, who was still at the Kerr Center, and he casually mentioned something about my ex-wife's recent marriage. I thought I had misunderstood him. I said, "What did you say?" Jack replied, "Yeah, Darla got married least week, at least that's what I heard. Didn't you know? Jack Witherow told me, and I think he went to the wedding." My interest skyrocketed. "Jack, get off the phone and ask Witherow to call me as soon as he can." It wasn't very long until the phone rang and Jack Witherow was on the line.

"Jack, what's this I hear about Darla getting married?"

"That's right, last Saturday. I didn't go to the wedding—Elizabeth did—but I went to the reception."

"Thank you very much," I said as I hung up the phone.

To confirm what I had heard, I called my son Curt. "Curt, I heard your mother got married, is this true?" There was a long pause. "Yeah that's true, Daddy. Mother told us not to tell you because she wanted to tell you herself." I thanked him and hung up thinking: I wonder when she was going to tell me?

This news meant that the alimony I was paying would stop. This was great news for me. It was like getting a big raise in my paycheck. Now I could start living more normally much sooner than I had expected. Happy day!

XII

My New Life

I was quite comfortable with my job and enjoyed living in the Washington, D.C. area. After I had been at EPA headquarters about a year, our office had a major reorganization. (In government it is common practice to reorganize at frequent intervals in order to hide the mistakes of the past and to shift responsibility for the mistakes of the future.) This reorganization divided our office into three sections responsible for drinking water and pesticides research, hazardous and solid wastes research, and industrial wastes and radiation research. I was put in charge of the Drinking Water and Pesticides Section. In this position I had more responsibility and had more interplay with the regulatory side of EPA. I also had a small staff to supervise.

Some time earlier I had met Mary Ellis at a government meeting, and we had had infrequent contact after our meeting. She worked for the Food and Drug Administration and had been District Director in the Puerto Rico District and was currently District Director in the Chicago District. She was originally from the Washington, D.C. area and still owned a home in Arlington. We started seeing each other more frequently on her trips back to Arlington and at other times.

Mary had been married for a number of years but was divorced. Her maiden name was Kiessling and was from a large family originally from Jackson, Michigan. She had five brothers and five sisters, she being the oldest girl but having two brothers her senior. During Mary's freshman year in college, the family moved to Huntington, WV, when her father's company transferred him to their plant there. Mary transferred to Marshall University in Huntington for her sophomore year and graduated from Marshall with a degree in chemistry. All of her five sisters were nurses—she said she couldn't stand the sight of blood so pursued another career.

As time went by, and we saw more of each other, we began to think about marriage. Mary was a highly intelligent, very sophisticated, and beautiful lady, and I was very much in love with her. In time she acknowledged her love for me—it took her a while.

Mary had had an outstanding government career. She was a biochemist with the Army at Fort Meade, Maryland, following her graduation from Marshall. She moved into the food chemistry area and fast-tracked to nuclear chemistry employing, at times, the new nuclear reactor at Walter Reed Army Institute of Research. The Food and Drug Administration needed her expertise, so in 1966 she moved into foods and later into the drugs area. She was placed in an executive development program in 1970 and soon began work on her Master's Degree in Government Administration at George Washington University, which was awarded in 1974. In 1978 she was the first woman appointed a District Director in the FDA—a real pioneering experience. Her position was District Director in the Puerto Rico District which included Puerto Rico and the U.S. Virgin Islands. In 1982 she was assigned as District Director of the Chicago District. The challenges of the Tylenol deaths in Chicago occurred shortly after her assignment there. Her handling of that incident brought lasting changes in the packaging of foods and drugs.

By mid-1984 we had decided to get married. After much shopping, Mary found the dress in Chicago that she wanted for the wedding, but she could not find a hat to go with it. This was the holdup to setting a wedding date. Mary said we would set the date only when she found the right hat to go with her dress. Time passed while Mary looked in store after store in Chicago and in the Washington area. Finally she gave up and had the hat made to her design by a hat maker. With this accomplished, our wedding was set for September 8, 1984.

Mary was also Catholic. We had both obtained church annulments of our first marriages, so we could be married in the church. We were married in St. Edmunds Catholic Church, the church Mary attended in the Chicago suburb of Oak Park, where she lived. The pastor, Father Kelly, celebrated the marriage. We have kept in touch with him through the years. In meeting with Father Kelly to plan the wedding, we told him that we wanted a nice small wedding. He summed it up exactly when he said, "Small but elegant." And it was.

Our attendants were Mary's sister Reita and her husband Charles. Mary's father gave her away. All of Mary's brothers and sisters and their spouses, except her sister Nancy and brother David, and some nephews and nieces attended. Considering the size of her family, this was a goodly number. I was represented by my daughter Darla Ann and my nephew Curtis Henry Covert and his wife. Darla Ann's arrival was a big surprise to me; Mary had secretly arranged for her to be there. Curtis Henry, my sister's oldest, had promised earlier that he would attend if and when we got married. He kept his word. We had a sit-down dinner at the local hotel following the ceremony, after which Mary and I departed for our honeymoon in San Diego.

After our week in the San Diego area, we returned to Chicago. We both still had jobs, Mary's in Chicago, mine in Washington. I returned to my apartment in Arlington; Mary remained in her apartment in Oak Park. For the next two years we maintained a long-distance marriage. We were together almost every weekend, one week Mary's traveling to Arlington, the next my traveling to Chicago. We racked up many frequent flyer miles. We also took advantage of the generous leave policies that our jobs offered so that we could be together. Our jobs kept us busy during the week, and the telephone was much used, so all things considered, it wasn't a bad arrangement.

One weekend, shortly after we were married, we were having breakfast in Mary's apartment when the telephone rang. The party on the line informed me that my sister, Hazel, had died; it was November 23, 1984. She had had a stroke and died on the way to the hospital. We immediately made airline reservations, flew to San Antonio where we rented a car, and drove to Kerrville where Hazel had lived and where the funeral would be. I was the only survivor of our immediate family. Following the funeral we returned to Chicago and Arlington to resume our routines.

Mary's house in Arlington had been rented, but in early 1985 it was vacant. It needed a lot of work before it could be rented again. We decided that I would move into it and start doing some of the things that it needed. In March 1985 I moved from my apartment to her house at 500 South 24th Street. I did a lot of painting, odd jobs, and yard work, and it was finally in pretty good shape.

We made good use of every minute of our time together. When Mary was in Washington, we very often went to concerts at the Kennedy Center. We made short trips to various places and visited family and friends. In Chicago we went to the theater and sometimes visited Mary's sister, Reita, and her family, who lived only a couple of hours away in Wisconsin. These were good times, which we thoroughly enjoyed.

By 1987 Mary had been in Chicago four years, and she was ready to retire. Her retirement date was January 1, 1987, after almost 37 years of government service. I gave her a retirement party in a hotel in Arlington, which many of her friends of long standing attended. We returned to Chicago for a retirement party given by her office.

Before Mary's retirement we began to think about the place we would live when we were together. We wanted to live in the Washington area, Mary had many friends there, and I was still working. We spent several weekends looking at places. We soon realized that any place that was close in was too expensive, and to find housing within our financial means meant we would have a long commute distance to and from Washington. Finally we decided that we could not have a more convenient location than Mary's house so why not spend what was needed to fix it up to our liking? So it was settled, we would live in Mary's house.

We hired an architect who drew plans that were not to our liking. Using them as a start, we developed our own plans to expand and upgrade the kitchen; remove interior walls between the kitchen, dining room, and living room; add a family room and a downstairs bathroom. Nothing was done to the three upstairs bedrooms and bath at that time. We hired a contractor and after much anguish the job was done. I soon embarked on a project to add a deck on the back adjacent to the new family room. I designed it and built it completely. I say without fear of contradiction, it was a work of art. We had a very comfortable home, which was open and good for entertaining.

I continued my job at EPA, although I was beginning to give some thoughts to retirement.

In August 1987 we attended a Harlan reunion celebrating the 300 years of the Harlans in America. It was held in New Castle, Delaware, which is where George and Michael landed in 1687, it then being in William Penn's Colony.[13] My niece, Hazel Marie Foltyn, and her father, also attended the reunion. There were about 800 in attendance from far and wide. It was a very interesting experience.

I retired April 1, 1988. I could not pass up that date—not only was it April Fool's Day, it was also Good Friday and Passover. Seldom do all three of these special days fall on the same day. I could not pass up the opportunity to work all

---

[13] See pages 3.

sides of the street. I was given a very nice retirement party by my office with several out-of-towners in attendance. Jim Kingery, from the Kerr Center, attended and presented me with a copy of a proclamation, signed by the mayor of Ada, proclaiming the day as Curtis Harlin Day in Ada, Oklahoma. This was a great surprise to me and something I have treasured.

In early August 1988 we took our first trip to France, spending most of the time in Paris and vicinity. The trip was with a group of Friends of the Corcoran Gallery of Washington, and since it was sponsored by the Corcoran Gallery, the itinerary concentrated on art galleries, museums, and cathedrals. In Paris we visited the Louvre, Notre Dame, Sainte Chapelle, the Eiffel Tower, Museum d'Orsay, and many more places of interest. Outside of Paris we traveled to Rouen, Chartres, Fontainebleau, Versailles, Barbizon, and the artist Monet's home Giverny. It was a wonderful trip and hooked us on France.

In the following years we made several trips to France, traveling on our own. Each trip we concentrated on a certain region. We would fly to Paris, rent a car and drive, or take a train, to our destination. We stayed in a hotel in a central city, and each day we would explore the region by car. From the City of Bordeaux we explored the Bordeaux Region, from Dijon we explored the Burgundy Region, and from Epernay we explored the Champaign Region. Our last trip was to the southern part of France where we divided our time between Perpignan, near the Spanish border, and Aix-en-Provence in the Marseille area. One day during this trip we visited Monaco, and on our return to Paris we spent a couple of days there. And yes, we went to Disneyland in France. We enjoyed France very much. The French people in Paris are not very cordial, but we found that outside of Paris the people are very friendly and helpful.

During our Dijon trip, we had a very unusual experience. Arriving at the Charles de Gaulle Airport in the morning, after picking up our checked bags, we took the elevator to the ground floor to pick up a rental car. The elevator was crowded, and our luggage cart was piled high with our bags, Mary's large traveling purse on the top. We secured our car and headed in the direction of Dijon on Route A6. At Chablis, about midway between Paris and Dijon, we decided to stop and spend the night. The six hours lost between the U.S. and France, and our sleepless night on the flight, was catching up with us. Checking into a hotel and bringing our bags in, Mary discovered that her purse was missing. We searched the car and our route from the car to our room and there was no sign of her purse. Her purse contained only a small amount of money, but her checkbook, credit cards, and driver's license were in it. Fortunately, it did not contain her passport; I always carry our passports in a special pouch that I keep on my person.

There seemed to be nothing we could do; just write the loss off as a bad experience and not let this incident spoil our trip. The next morning, after a restful night, we proceeded to Dijon. We had a very enjoyable time the next few days in the Dijon area. One day we visited a World War I military cemetery at Meuse-Argonne. We always visit these cemeteries when we are in the neighborhood of one. They are immaculate, and they give us a feeling of pride for the sacrifices made for our country. While in the cemetery talking to the manager, who was American, Mary mentioned the loss of her purse. The manager said that purse-snatching was quite common, usually done by young Gypsies operating in crowded places. He said that they were interested only in money, but if the purses contained little money they would turn the purses in for, hopefully, a reward.

Upon completing our trip we arrived back at de Gaulle Airport for our flight home. We were at the airport early and had quite a wait before our flight time. Remembering what the cemetery manager had told us—if purses contained very little money they would be turned in—Mary said, "I think

I'll go to the lost and found and see if my purse was turned in." As she left, I thought, *silly girl.*

In a very few minutes she came rushing back.

"My purse was turned in, but it is at the police station in the city. Give me some money so I can take a cab to go get it."

I reached into my pocket, retrieved a handful of francs, handed them to her, and off she ran.

I had no idea how far it was to the police station in the city or how long it would take to get there. While we had a considerable length of time before our flight, as time passed, and it got nearer to our departure time—and no Mary—I began to worry. With only a few minutes left before our boarding time, in came Mary clutching the missing purse.

She had had quite a harrowing experience. Upon arriving at the police station, she could not make the police understand her problem. The cab driver spoke fairly good English so she went out to the cab to solicit his help. He had no trouble telling the police what the problem was, and after paying the police a few francs Mary had her purse. With time running short, the cab driver returned to the airport in record time. Mary was fortunate that the cab driver spoke English and graciously helped her. Upon examining the contents of her purse, she discovered that the few dollars that she had had was all that was missing. The most important items—credit cards, checkbook, driver's license—were still there. This experience showed us that even in Paris, there are some very nice people.

From every trip to France we brought back an experience that we will always remember, like the time in the Burgundy Region that we visited with the elderly lady living in an old monastery, surrounded by her vineyard. I don't know how we found this place, but when we drove into the yard we thought the place was abandoned. We were just about to drive away when the lady came out of the building. We got out of the car and introduced ourselves. We learned that she lived there alone and produced wine from her small vineyard. We spent the next hour, with her broken English and our even more broken French, hearing her fascinating story of how the vineyard had been in her family many many years, how she made and bottled her wine alone in the old monastery that she lived in, and that she had sons who had larger vineyards in the region.

Another unforgettable experience, in the Bordeaux Region, was the day we spent in the village of Saint Emilion, one of the principal red wine areas of Bordeaux. As early as the 2nd century, AD, the Romans planted vineyards in this area. The town dates from the 8th century when Emilion came and established his hermitage, which was carved in the limestone that underlies the area. We visited his abode, which is not much larger than an area for a person to sit in, hardly large enough for an average person to lie down in. No wonder he was declared a saint. The monolithic church, carved out in a limestone cliff was another point of interest. Of course, we treated ourselves to their great wine at a lunch table in an outdoor café, which we shared with a young couple who were backpacking around Europe.

The time we were treated like royalty at Epernay in the Champagne region of France remains in our memories. We were taking a tour of the Moett & Chandon Champagne winery with a group of eight or ten visitors, when, for some reason, we mentioned that the year before we had visited their sister winery in California and were members of their Chandon Club. Immediately, the tour guide pulled us out of the group, turned the tour over to another guide, and escorted Mary and me into a great room in the center of which was a large table, as found in a cooperation board room, and an elaborate bar. For the next hour the three of us sat at the table and our host plied us with champagne and goodies. After awhile Mary said, apologetically, "We don't want to keep you from your job." His quick response was, "You are my job." We were treated as CEOs of major cooperations or high level government dignitaries instead of members of an unexclusive club that all you have to do to join is give your name and address. We thoroughly enjoyed the time.

I had been retired about three months when I received a call from my former office director asking me if I would come back to help out on a project. This was not entirely unexpected because I had talked to him about working part-time after I retired. I was hired as a part-time consultant to work three day a week, and I started working on a very interesting project. I was an EPA representative on a joint project with the Departments of Energy and Defense. I set my own schedule, and from time to time briefed the office director, and other EPA managers, on project activities. I really enjoyed the work. Unlike my positions before my retirement, I had no supervisory responsibilities, wasn't bothered with all the time-wasting telephone calls, and didn't have to attend all of those worthless meetings.

The last weekend in October 1988 Mary and I attended a wedding of one of her nieces in Kentucky. On returning home that Sunday, I received a telephone call from my son-in-law in Oklahoma.

He said, "Dad are you sitting down?"

"No," I answered.

His response was, "You had better sit down; I have some bad news."

"What is it?"

"Curt is dead."

What can one say when he just received the unexpected news that his only son had died? It took some time for me to recover enough from the initial shock to ask for details. It seemed that Curt had shot himself. Curt kept a gun in his pharmacy because he had had some problems with burglars who were after narcotics that pharmacies stock. So I knew that he had access to a gun. I was not told, completely, the details of the event at that time.

177

Mary and I flew to Dallas the next day, rented a car, and drove to Ada where the funeral would be held. Curt lived in Valliant, Oklahoma, where his pharmacy was located, but he and his wife had divorced before his death. His mother and sister lived in Ada, and he had grown up there, so it was logical that he be buried there. The funeral was conducted in the First Baptist Church, the church he had attended for so many years, and he was buried in the Ada cemetery. He died October 29, 1988, being 37 years old, leaving a seven-year-old daughter, Heather. The police ruled the death a suicide. After hearing the circumstance, however, I am convinced that Curt was clowning around, as he so often did, and did not intend to shoot himself. However, with the evidence the police had, I can understand that their only conclusion could be suicide. The loss of Curt is the saddest event of my life.

In August 1989 Mary and I took our first cruise together. Mary had taken a Caribbean cruise on the Queen Elizabeth II several years earlier, and I had cruised the Mediterranean many years before, but this was our first cruise together. We boarded the Island Princess at Vancouver and sailed the Inland Passage to Anchorage, Alaska, stopping at Ketchikan, Juneau, and Skagway. After flying from Anchorage to Fairbanks, where we stayed a couple of days, we took a train to Denali Park for an overnight. After a day in Denali Park, we continued our train ride to Anchorage for our return flight home.

We were hooked on cruising. In the years following we took many cruises, some years two cruises. We cruised the Baltic with visits to Denmark, Finland, Sweden, and Russia; from Santiago, Chili, we sailed around the cape to Buenos Aries; from Barcelona, Spain, to England with stops in Normandy; the French Polynesia with stops at the various islands including Tahiti and Bora Bora; through the Panama Canal; numerous Caribbean cruises; and others that are lost to my memory.

XIII

Retirement

With Mary retired and my working only part-time, we had plenty of time for travel and other activities. We became active in Our Lady of Lourdes Church, which was only three blocks from our home.

In November 1988, Mary and I took a trip to England, primarily to visit the old Monkwearmouth Monastery that had played an important role in the Harland family in early years.[14] After flying into London we rented a car and headed north. We had heard so much about the bread-and-breakfast establishments in England that we planned to stay in them during this trip. The night of November 8 we were staying in a B&B in Durham, owned by a young couple who also made it their home. Early in the evening we went to the Durham Cathedral where we enjoyed a Vespers, which featured a large boys' choir. Construction of the cathedral was started in 1093, and it is still used as a house of worship today. It is considered one of the finest examples of a Norman cathedral in Europe, and in 1986 UNESCO designated it a World Heritage Site. The pageantry and singing that evening was outstanding.

November 8 was Presidential Election Day that year in the United States, and we were interested in the outcome. George Herbert Walker Bush was the 1988 Republican presidential candidate, and his running mate was Dan Quayle, U.S. Senator from Indiana. The Democrats

---

[14] See Chapter I, page 2.

nominated Michael Dukakis, governor of Massachusetts, as their candidate with Lloyd Bentsen his running mate.

On returning to our B&B from the cathedral, we turned on the television and found, to our delight, that BBC was carrying our election results. We settled down to watch, and, to our surprise, the owners of the B&B joined us. Because of the time difference, we didn't stay up to hear the final results, but we didn't retire until after two o'clock in the morning. Our hosts stayed up the entire time and seemed as interested in the results as we were. The next day we learned that our candidate, Bush, had won.

January 1989, Mary received a birthday present that we have both enjoyed ever since—a little ball of fur that we named Heidi. Mary's birthday fell on a Sunday that year, and Reita and Charles came to celebrate with us. Upon arriving, they presented Mary with a shoebox with a decorative red bow on top. When she opened it—Surprise! Surprise! —out came an adorable 10-week-old Schnauzer puppy. Mary had had dogs before and loved them, but it had been several years since she had one. Reita had talked to me earlier about giving Mary a puppy for Christmas. I discouraged it, because we did a lot of traveling and I thought it wouldn't be a good idea to have a dog. They didn't give Mary a dog for Christmas, but when her birthday came January 29, since I had not spoken to the subject of a dog-present for her birthday, I guess they thought it would be OK. We immediately fell in love with Heidi, and she became the third member of our family. Through the years she has brought us much enjoyment, and as I write this she is now 17 years old. She is totally deaf and blind and has a heart condition that we medicate her for, but we love her dearly.

The year 1990 was a year for the presentation of the world famous Passion Play in Oberammergau, Germany, and Mary and I signed up for a tour that included going to see the play and other points of interest in Europe. We boarded an Iceland Air flight in Baltimore, Maryland, June 21. We made a refueling stop in Reykjavik, Iceland, and landed in Luxembourg about noon June 22. Our group was small and we traveled in a small bus, which made the tour very comfortable and enjoyable. We visited Trier, Koblenz, and Frankfurt, before arriving at Oberammergau. Because of the multitudes that attend the passion play, accommodations in Oberammergau are filled early. We were housed in a nice quaint hotel in the picturesque town of Garmisch, not far from Oberammergau. We will never forget being awakened in the mornings by the tinkling of cowbells as the cows were herded through the town's streets to pasture for the day. The play was wonderful—a lifetime experience. On our return trip we visited Munich, Heidelberg, and Luxembourg. This was a great trip.

In October 1990 we went on a trip to the British Isles with a group from Our Lady of Lourdes Church, led by Fr. Rippy. We toured England, Ireland, Wales, and Scotland. It was an enjoyable trip and the first of three trips we took with the church group. We followed this trip with trips to Italy and Spain.

In Italy, we visited Venice, Florence, Milan, Pieza, Assisi, and Rome. Fr. Rippy conducted mass each morning, sometimes in very interesting places. In Assisi, we had mass in the old church of Saint Francis. A year or two after we were there they had an earthquake that did extensive damage to the church.

Our trip to Spain was one of the most interesting. We flew to Madrid where we spent some time touring the city. By bus we visited Cordoba, Seville, Granada, and other points of interest in Spain. One of the most interesting places we visited was the Alhambra in Granada. This large citadel was built by the Moorish rulers in the 13th and 14th centuries. It is truly an architectural marvel. Spain today, especially the southern part, still shows heavy Moorish influence. The Moors conquered most of the Iberian peninsular in the 8th century, and established their capital at Cordoba. By the beginning of the 16th century, the Moorish influence had been largely replaced by Christianity.

While in Spain we crossed the Strait of Gibraltar and visited Gibraltar and Casablanca in Morocco. We saw the monkeys on the rocks of Gibraltar. The English, who own Gibraltar, say that as long as the monkeys are on Gibraltar, the English will be there too. I was first introduced to couscous in a restaurant in Casablanca. We bought two area rugs in the bazaar of Casablanca and had them shipped home.

We proceeded to Portugal and spent some time in Lisbon. Other than Lisbon, and the country side as we went to and from Lisbon from Spain, we saw very little of Portugal. We saw enough to recognize that Portugal was a very poor country. I also saw the oak trees that produce cork. Until then I didn't know that cork was produced from the bark of an oak.

After these trips we decided that we would enjoy our traveling more by ourselves. Not that we didn't enjoy the trips with the church group, but sometimes having to abide by others' schedules, and the inevitable complaints, didn't sit very well with us. In the following years we did extensive travel—just the two of us—in Europe as well as the United States.

Two trips to Europe are remembered as especially enjoyable: Holland in 1992 and Austria in 1996. Through some friends, we heard of a bike and barge trip in Holland, which sounded interesting and different. After receiving detailed information about it, we decided to go. We flew to Amsterdam in April and boarded the barge that would be our home for the next ten days. The barges accommodated only 24 passengers and, while they were certainly not luxurious, they provided all of the necessities. There was a kitchen and dining room, where we had most of our meals, and a lounge where we would congregate in the evening to discuss the adventures we had that day. Being such a small group, we became very friendly and congenial.

In preparation for the trip, I went into training. I bought a new 10-speed bicycle and all of the accessories that the salesperson said a respectable bike rider needed; I started riding on the bike path that passed near our home. I soon found out that I was far from being in condition for any heavy-duty riding, but I did my rides regularly until the day of our departure.

Each morning the bikers would leave the barge, ride through the countryside, and meet the barge at the end of the day at a different location. During the day the barge would travel the canals and rivers, stopping at points of interest, and enjoying the scenery. Those who stayed on the barge were treated to as much, or more, of the countryside, and what it had to offer, as the bikers. Plus, they didn't have to exert themselves, to enjoy the day, to the extent the bikers did. A couple of weeks before our trip, Mary had had a bad fall and had seriously injured her ankle. For several days we thought we would have to cancel our trip. We finally decided that we could go, but Mary would not do any bicycle riding. This turned out fine, and she enjoyed the trip as much as I did.

I had not ridden a bicycle in years before the trip. In the information we received about the trip was the itinerary, which gave the distance of the daily bike rides. The first day the route would be 70 kilometers (40 miles), the longest that was scheduled. Other days the rides were 20 to 30 miles. I knew that I could never do the 40-mile ride, and I had my doubts about a 20-mile ride.

The first morning on the barge, after breakfast, the bikers assembled on deck and checked out their bicycles. After inspecting them, they mounted them and were off. As if in a hypnotic trance, I checked out a bicycle, inspected it, mounted it, and was off with the group. A few pedals down the road I suddenly thought: What am I doing on this thing? In my training program in Arlington, the farthest I had peddled in one trip was probably not more that three or four miles. As I continued with the group, I didn't experience the fatigue that I had anticipated; in fact with each mile I felt renewed energy from some mysterious source.

The beauty of the landscape may have been responsible for keeping my mind off the strain of the peddling. The fields of tulips and other flowers were alive with color, row after row of reds, yellows, blues, as far as the eyes could see in every direction. We were viewing these picture postcard scenes during the peak of the season. The terrain was table flat, nothing obscured the view—it was mesmerizing.

At the end of the day, when we met up with the barge, my muscles felt the wear and tear of the ride, but I was not exhausted, in fact I felt pretty good. But the next morning was a different story—getting out of bed was a project. I stayed on the barge the next day, my excuse being that it was raining. In fact it rained some nearly every day of the trip, but this didn't deter most of the riders. I probably rode half of the days.

On our return home, we could truly say that this was undoubtedly the most colorful trip we had ever made. The beauty of Holland in the springtime is unsurpassed.

In June 1996 Mary and I flew to Vienna. We checked into a small hotel, which was convenient to shops and public transportation. We soon found that Vienna was very pedestrian-friendly and could easily be toured without a car. We picked up maps that outlined excellent walking tours, which, if followed, one could see most of the major attractions of the city in a couple of days. This we did.

Vienna is a fascinating city of about a million and a half population. Its importance in European history is profound; having been the center of power of the Habsburg Empire, which by the late 19th century included all of central Europe. The magnificent St. Stephen's Cathedral, in the center of the city, dominates the skyline; its soaring tower can be seen throughout the city. The city is filled with palaces, churches, museums, opera houses, and concert halls; parks and gardens are everywhere. In our two-day stay we didn't see everything, but we didn't miss much.

Leaving Vienna we traveled by train to the city of Klagenfurt southwest of Vienna in the Lake District. Our purpose for stopping there was to pick up a rental car to drive to our destination for the week, the small town of Villach, where we had reserved a time-share apartment. Villach is in the southern part of Austria, only a short distance from the Italian border, surrounded by natural beauty—forests, mountains, streams—and quaint villages and country churches. Each day we would explore the countryside and were always delighted by what we found over the next hill or around the next bend in the road. One day, in our wanderings, we arrived in Klagenfurt and discovered a very unusual and interesting attraction called *Minimundus*. It is a lakeside park containing scale models of important and famous buildings from around the world. Several were from the United States, including the White House and the Statue of Liberty. We spent a very fascinating couple of hours there.

At the end of our week in the Villach area, we turned in our car and boarded the train in Klagenfurt for Salzburg. The train ride took most of the day, but it was not wasted time. The ride through the Alps was spectacular, and being on a train there was nothing to obscure the beauty of the forests, streams, and mountains. Arriving in Salzburg in the late afternoon, we checked into our hotel.

Every place we went we were reminded that Salzburg was the birthplace of Mozart—street names, parks, restaurants—his name was on everything. One day we took a tour of the area, which included the locations where much of *The Sound of Music* was filmed. We were told that the people of Salzburg were not very enthused about the film. Evidently they felt that parts of the film didn't show Salzburg in a very good light. Salzburg is a very interesting city with lots of history and culture. Our two days there were somewhat dampened, as it rained the entire time. We were told that rain was common that time of year.

After our two days in Salzburg, we boarded the train to return to Vienna. The ride to Vienna was not as spectacular as through the mountains when we traveled from Klagenfurt to Salzburg; the countryside was not as mountainous and wooded, more agricultural, but it was an enjoyable ride. After an overnight in Vienna, our flight returned us home. This trip was truly one we would treasure in years to come.

We enjoyed the convenience of the location of our home in Arlington, but there were features of the house that we wanted to improve and additions that we would like to make. This isn't to say that the house was not comfortable for two—excuse me, for three, I forgot Heidi. Our previous remodeling job had opened up the house and made it quite livable. One feature, not to our liking, was that we had no breakfast eating area; we ate in the kitchen. This had not been too bad before Heidi, but the kitchen had also become Heidi's bedroom. From her beginning with us she had slept in her crate. During the first months this was for training, but as she grew older it became only her bed at night. She never went in the crate in the daytime, but when bedtime came she just automatically went to her bed, the crate, which was in the kitchen.

After we agonized over the alternatives for months, I put pencil to paper and came up with some plans. In time we refined them to our satisfaction and submitted them to the Arlington County building permit department. Because the design extended over our lot's building line by a little over a foot, we had to apply for a variance. In a month or so our hearing was scheduled before the planning board. Because there was no opposition voiced from the neighbors, and because of my brilliant presentation to the board, the variance was approved. We were then ready to talk to a contractor—and our banker.

We hired the same contractor who had done the previous remodeling, and the work was started. The work seemed to us to proceed as a small spirally coiled shelled *Gastropoda*. The house was covered with dust, in spite of the precautions the contractor made, and at times the kitchen was almost unusable. But it was a difficult job and in retrospect I feel that the contractor did an excellent job. In time the job was completed and we were enjoying a new bay-windowed morning room off the kitchen, and a new bedroom, additional closet space, and an additional bathroom upstairs. The inconvenience and dust had been worth it.

About this time we became interested in collecting art. Our introduction to the art world was when we attended an art auction that was sponsored by a charity that one of my colleagues at work was interested in. Before the evening was over we had bid on, and bought, probably seven or eight framed pictures, some of dubious quality. During the evening, when Mary had gone to the ladies' room, I was doing a lot of bidding. One of our friends went to the ladies' room and said to Mary, "You should come out here, Curtis is bidding on everything." Mary showed no interest, for at that moment she was kneeling on the floor looking for her lost pearls. The string of a pearl bracelet that I had recently bought for her had broken and she was franticly searching for the pearls on the floor of the ladies' restroom. At that moment her valuable pearls were worth much more to her than any cheap artwork I was buying. Her diligence paid off—she found every one of the pearls. Shortly thereafter she had them restrung with knots between each pearl.

When we got our new art acquisitions home we had no interest in most of them. A gallery from Philadelphia conducted the auction, and they had stated that any art we bought at the auction could be traded at their gallery. We made a trip to their gallery and traded most of our pictures for a large Don Hatfield serigraph. There were a couple of the ones we originally bought that we kept. This experience indicated that I was a sucker for art auctions; this was the beginning of our acquiring a very nice collection of art including serigraphs, lithographs, and original pieces.

Our home was on a large corner lot in the Crystal City area of Arlington. We were in the first block of a residential area that extended west from Eads Street for a number of blocks. Across Eads Street was commercial, dominated by hotels and office buildings. Keeping the large yard in acceptable condition was a real struggle. We had remodeled the house, making it very attractive and comfortable, now it was time to work on the yard.

We approached Bill Allen, a friend of ours who did gardening, about doing our yard. He was also our dance instructor—but that is another story. He started to work putting in place, with some modifications, a design that we had had a landscape architect prepare for our yard. You can't have instant results with this kind of project, but by the second year our yard was beginning to be a showplace, all kinds of flowers and shrubs dominating both front and back yards. Bill worked as a volunteer at the National Arboretum in Washington. From time to time they would clean out beds at the Arboretum and replant them. Often he would bring some of the discarded plants to our yard; consequently, we had exotic plants that could not be seen in most homeowners' yards. In the next few years our yard was truly a show place; people walking by our house would stop to admire its beauty. I did the grass mowing; Bill was interested only in planting and maintaining the flowerbeds and pruning the trees and shrubs.

The back 20 to 30 feet of our lot was outside of the fenced area that kept Heidi in, so I used this area for my vegetable garden. I always planted tomatoes and peppers, which did quite well, and in the beginning various other vegetables such as beans, squash, and cucumbers. Mary loves raspberries, so I consented to plant some of the berries in my garden. The six raspberry plants that I planted have an interesting story.

Years ago, Mary's father had a large patch of raspberries in Huntington, West Virginia. Every year he harvested enough to sell, even after he and his wife had plenty for themselves. His berries were in such demand that, during the season, people called and came by the home to get the berries. The demand was greater than his supply. Through the years he gave a start of plants to his children, including a son who lived in Cincinnati. This son in time gave a start of plants to a brother who lived in Indianapolis. As time passed, the brother in Indianapolis gave plants to his sister and brother-in-law who lived in York, Pennsylvania. When I decided to start raspberries, I turned to the brother-in-law in York, who is my brother-in-law too, for a start of plants. I was given six plants but only four survived the traumatic experience of being uprooted in York, Pennsylvania, and moved to Arlington, Virginia.

I had never grown raspberries and knew nothing about their habits. I didn't know their propensity to multiply and occupy all of the space around them. In a few years, our raspberry patch expanded until it occupied the largest part of my garden space, leaving space for only tomatoes and peppers. Incidentally, I gave a start of raspberry plants to my brother-in-law—Mary's youngest brother—who lives in South Carolina. And so, as Johnny Appleseed did with apple seeds, Mary's family did with raspberries—spread them around the country.

As to our dancing career, it started when Mary and I enrolled in a beginners' ballroom dance group class conducted by the Arlington County Recreation Department. Bill Allen was the instructor. Bill had earned his spurs as an instructor with the Author Murray dance studio and, in addition to being an excellent teacher, had a most likeable personality. We completed the beginners' class, which was followed by an advanced class that we also completed. The county didn't offer any additional ballroom classes. To advance beyond the beginners' stage one had to go to a private dance studio. We learned that Bill worked for the Tom Wohl Dance Studio, so we signed up for private lessons. We took one-hour classes once a week.

As time went on and we began to develop confidence, we joined the Capitol Cotillion Club, which held dinner dances once a month. This was a formal group with very strict dress code: black tie required for the gentlemen, formal evening gowns for the ladies. We enjoyed being in this group and we made many friends. We became quite good with foxtrot, waltz, swing, rumba, cha-cha, and other Latin dances. Before Bill moved to Colorado we had had ten years of private ballroom dance lessons.

In the early days of our dancing, there were not many ballroom dancers. When we went on cruises, sometimes we would be the only couple on the dance floor. Through the years ballroom dancing has really caught on; now everyone is doing it. On recent cruises we have found the dance floors usually crowded, a big change in the past 15 years. Dancing is like everything else; if you don't use it you lose it. We still dance but not as frequently as in the past, and we haven't had any lessons in eight or nine years. My dancing skills have suffered. Mary remains a very good dancer, but I am not the leader I once was.

One of the most unique and enjoyable Christmases we have had was spent in Thornbury Castle in England. Thornbury Castle, located in the village of Thornbury, a short distance from Bristol, was built by the 3rd Duke of Buckingham in the early 1500s. In 1521 the duke was accused of treason and was beheaded by order of King Henry VIII. Thornbury Castle was then seized by Henry VIII and was a Royal Demesen for the next 33 years. In 1535 the king stayed in the castle with Anne Boleyn for ten days. Mary Tudor lived in the castle for a number of years before becoming Queen. In 1554 the Queen returned the property to the descendants of the original owner, the Duke of Buckingham.

One Sunday, while reading the Travel Section of the *Washington Times*, I ran across an article written about a couple's Christmas in an English Castle, hosted by the owner, The Baron of Portlethen. The article included the name and address and telephone number of the castle: Thornbury Castle. In the next few days I made a call to the castle and was informed that the castle would be closed the next Christmas, because the Baron and his family would be using it. I was told that it would be open the following Christmas, and we were put on their mailing list. During the next few months we had frequent correspondence with the manager of the castle, which culminated in booking our Christmas of 1997 in Thornbury Castle.

December 22, 1997, we boarded a Virgin Atlantic Airline plane at Washington Dulles Airport for an overnight flight to London's Heathrow Airport, arriving early the next morning. To recuperate from our overnight flight, we spent the night in London. The next day we took a train from Paddington Station to the Bristol Parkway Station, an hour and a half trip. On arriving at the station we were met by a driver named Roger who whisked us to the castle, a 30-minute drive.

The castle appeared to look the same as it probably looked 500 years before— surrounded by its high walls, gardens, and its vineyard. We were welcomed by the manager and assigned our room—or bedchamber, as the English say. What a room, it was gigantic! It could almost accommodate a basketball court. It was on the second floor and had two huge fireplaces and private bath. The view from the windows on one side was of the walled garden, while from the windows on the other side there was a view of the vineyard. The furniture was elegant and reminiscent of Tudor times. One could easily get lost in the huge canopied bed.

That early evening, which was Christmas Eve, we met in the courtyard to hear the Thornbury Brass Band play carols around a Christmas tree, while sipping mulled wine. We were then given time to dress for the welcoming "Black Tie" Champagne Reception in the private sitting room of the

Baron. We got acquainted, introducing ourselves and telling a little about where we were from, etc. The Baron and his wife, their son The Younger, and his wife and their adorable little son were very friendly and cordial. There were probably a total of 10 or 12 guests from many places. Our reception was followed by a five-course dinner and musical entertainment.

That night most of the guests went to Midnight Mass at the Church of England, which adjoined the castle property. Mary and I were the only ones who went to the Roman Catholic Church in the village. We stood out in the congregation, Mary in her fancy party dress and me in my tuxedo. The local folks were casually dressed, some in their work clothes. Everyone returned to the castle for mince pie and hot toddies before retiring. It was a wonderful start with much more to come.

Christmas morning we were served breakfast in our rooms after which we all met around the Christmas tree to open our Christmas gifts. We all received several gifts, all of which were quite nice. One of the gifts I received was a very nice silk tie; another we received was a nicely framed picture of the castle. After we had all opened our gifts, the Baron gave a talk on the history of Thornbury Castle, while we sipped sherry. At one o'clock we had our Christmas "Feast" with all the trimmings.

In the afternoon, following our feast, we embarked on a "Tudor Quest." This involved searching the castle and the grounds for a mysterious lost jewel, which it was believed, was hidden in the Castle. The jewel was not found, but it gave us all an opportunity to explore the Castle and its surroundings. In the evening we met again for cocktails and an informal light supper.

On Boxing Day, December 26, after breakfast, we walked into the village where the locals were gathering for the traditional foxhunt. The participitants, all dressed in their riding habits, were on their horses with the foxhounds swarming around the horses anxious for the hunt. To one side in a cage was a small Norfolk terrier, which is used by the hunters to ferret out foxes from their holes. The dog-lover Mary is, she kneeled down to give the cute little thing a pet. As she stuck her hand out, the dog, teeth bared and growling, made a snap at her hand. He let her know that he was not a petting dog but a working dog. It was like a movie scene when the hunters and dogs took off into the countryside for a day of fox hunting.

At 11:30 AM we traveled to "The Windbound Pub," which was owned by the Baron, located on the Severn River about seven miles from the castle. The Severn River separates England from Wales, which we could see from the pub. We were served the traditional Ploughman's Lunch of fresh crusty country bread, cheeses, and chutney, washed down with English Ale. We returned to the castle for four o'clock High Tea with an open discussion of English history. In the evening Chef Steven Black served an "Olde English" Christmas dinner.

The next morning after breakfast, we traveled to the Georgian city of Bath. We had free time for sightseeing and shopping before we assembled at 2:00 PM at the Theatre Royal for the pantomine *Aladdin*. Returning to the castle we got ready for our black tie farewell "Gala Dinner."

The following morning Roger took us to the train station and we said farewell to the Baron, his family, other guests, and Thornburg Castle. Arriving home the evening of December 29, we felt that the past few days had been a dream. It is doubtful that we will ever have a Christmas to equal this one.

I continued working three days a week at EPA, and although my duties had changes from time to time, I still enjoyed my work. Mary and I had plenty of time for travel and dancing and other activities. Our lives were very enjoyable. One thing did bother us though, that was the growing traffic and congestion in the Washington D.C. area. Our home was located on Eads Street, which is a major north-south thoroughfare connecting Alexander to the Pentagon area and Interstate 95. The next street east of Eads is Jefferson Davis Highway—Route One—which is a major north-south route into Washington. The noise and congestion from the increasing traffic on these streets was beginning to be a problem for us. How long would it be before we had had enough?

XIV

Our Move to Myrtle Beach

In the mid-1990s, we began to have thoughts of moving from Arlington. We enjoyed much of the Washington area, but the traffic, noise, and congestion was becoming a problem. We didn't want to completely leave the area, so, initially, we thought of buying a place in Florida, where we would spend the winters, returning to our home in Arlington for the summers. We would establish Florida as our residence because there was no income tax there. During this time we made a couple of trips to Florida, the Orlando and St. Petersburg areas, and while there we looked at property. We finally decided that Florida was not for us, so we turned our attention to other places.

We had vacationed several springs in Myrtle Beach, South Carolina, and had looked at properties there. On one visit we stopped at a development that had hardly gotten off the ground but had a temporary sales office on the site. It was conveniently located, but at that time we could tell nothing about it, as the streets were not even graded out. The next spring, when we visited Myrtle Beach, this development—called Charleston Place—had begun to take shape: streets were paved and a few houses had been built. We liked what we saw but didn't take any action.

On our visit to Myrtle Beach in April 1999, we decided to take the plunge: we made a deposit on a lot in Charleston Place. One of the attractions was the beach—Mary loved the beach. Myrtle Beach seemed to be a nice quiet town, and the weather was mild yet had seasons. It had good medical facilities, an active Catholic Church convenient to the development, theaters and other entertainment attractions, and Mary's brother David and his wife Sandy lived in Florence, only a couple of hours' drive. We thought this would be a good place to spend our waning years.

One could not buy a lot in Charleston Place and hold it; you had to start construction on a house within a year of purchasing a lot. The developer had eight or ten house plans that were being built in the subdivision. We liked some features of the plans, but we didn't like any one of them totally. The developer said we could make any changes that we wanted—for a price. Over the next several weeks we developed, in our minds and on pieces of paper, the plan we wanted and made several trips to Myrtle Beach to meet with the developer. On our return home each time, the developer would send us copies of the plans that supposedly included the ideas we had discussed with him. Invariably, they did not include all of what we wanted. After several attempts to develop the plans to our liking, the developer arranged a meeting with the architect. I went over every detail with the architect in his office; the next set of plans we received was what we wanted. If we had met with the architect in the beginning, instead of going through the middleman, we would not have gone through seven revisions of the plans.

On July 28, 1999, we signed a contract to start construction of our home. In the months following we made trips to Myrtle Beach every two or three weeks. Sometimes I would go alone, and sometimes Mary and I would both go. Since David and Sandy lived in the area, we would visit them on our trips (great lodging and good food). I must say that the construction went very well—no major problems—although it seemed to take a very long time.

With our new home under construction, we had a house in Arlington to sell. Real estate was selling very well in the Arlington area, and because we thought our house would sell fast, we were not in a hurry to put it on the market. We didn't want to sell our home in Arlington before our Myrtle

Beach home was completed. After talking to several Realtors we settled on one, and our house was put on the market. To our surprise, after six months our house had not sold. Since we had a six-month contract with the Realtor and because we were not pleased with the way he had performed, we changed Realtors.

After the Realtor's first look at our house, he said we had too much furniture: he thought it would show better if we removed some. Also, he strongly recommended that we remove all of the small items in the house that might be tempting for people to put in their pockets or purses, or which could be accidentally broken when showing the house. Mary is a collector, and she has many beautiful items such as Hummels, Lladros, and Herands, mostly breakable, and some quite valuable.

We rented a U-Haul truck and loaded it with small pieces of furniture and boxes of things from our basement. David had agreed that we could store our surplus things in his garage, so we headed the U-Haul in the direction of Florence. The stuff that we unloaded in his garage took most of one side of his two-car garage. On our frequent trips to check on the progress of our house, we took small items in the car that we added to our cache in the garage.

We still hadn't removed Mary's collectables; they had to be carefully packed and handled. On one of our trips to Myrtle Beach David suggested that we take his pickup truck and bring back these delicate pieces. This seemed like a good ideas, so when we returned home we started packing the items. Soon after packing them all, I took the Amtrak from Virginia to Florence to get David's pickup. This was the start of quite an experience.

The pickup was a small red Chevrolet with a hard cover on the bed. It had been used by David and Sandy's daughter, Amy, and it had its limitations. Foremost of these was its lack of air conditioning. It did have an air conditioner, but the air conditioner didn't work. This was definitely a problem when hitting the highway in 100-degree July temperature. To compound the problem, the air vent on the driver's side would not stay open. Every few minutes it would slam shut, cutting off fresh air from the outside. While trying to keep the machine in the proper lane of the road, the driver had to bend down across the steering wheel and reopen the vent. Just about the time the driver was once again enjoying the fresh outside air—WHAM! The vent would close again. The first few times this happened I had some exciting experiences with the pickup's drifting out of my traffic lane. I soon got the hang of it, and it became just routine. Since the radio didn't work either, having to tend to the vent every few miles kept the driver awake.

After about nine hours of coaxing the little red demon down I-95 I arrived safely in Florence. The next day I deposited my precious cargo in the garage, after which our allotted half was about filled to capacity. I warned David that I would refuse to borrow from him again unless he upgraded his equipment. (Several years later he did upgrade by buying a double cab Ford pickup with all the luxuries, including radio and air conditioner that worked.) I enjoyed a nice leisurely ride back home on the Amtrak.

As the year 2000 approached, there was much excitement and worry about what would happen when the clock struck midnight, ushering in the New Year and a new millennium. Those of certain Christian groups were sure that it would usher in the "last days" and urged everyone to "prepare for the coming of the Lord." The greatest secular concern was how industry, transportation, and communication systems, which were computer controlled, would react. Computer systems had had no trouble adjusting to the next year, but these systems had never been asked to automatically change from a 1900 date to a 2000 date. Would they properly recognize this change?

Widely published opinions predicted that trains and airplanes would stop, electric generating plants would shut down, telephone and other communication systems would be disrupted—transportation, industry, and even private lives would be in total chaos was the prediction. Industrial and communication systems prepared for these eventualities months in advance. Many individuals stocked groceries and water, bought electric generators, stashed large sums of cash where they would have access to it, and prepared alternative heating systems for their homes. As January 1, 2000, approached, many people were almost in a state of hysteria. Mary and I took this all in stride and took no unusual precautions. New Years Eve 1999 we were at home watching the happenings around the world on television when the clock struck midnight. When we were sure that nothing catastrophic was going to take place, we wished each other Happy New Year and went to bed.

In March 2000, after eight months in the building, our home in Myrtle Beach was completed. It had seemed like a long time in the making, but the builder had told us at the start that it would take about nine ninths. March 21, 2000, after a walkthrough inspection, Mary and I closed the deal. The house was beautiful and without any furniture in it, it looked huge. It was a good-size house, about the largest in the subdivision at 2700 square feet. We were happy with our home, but then we had two homes, as our house in Arlington had not sold.

In the next few weeks we divided our time between Arlington and Myrtle Beach. We had to spend some time in Myrtle Beach because the house there was now ours, and the yard and other things had to be taken care of. We met our neighbors during this time and got to know the neighborhood. Early in August, after a year on the market, our house in Arlington was sold to a Lt. Colonel and his wife, the colonel being transferred from Montgomery, Alabama, to the Pentagon

We arranged for movers to load our furniture early in the week of August 14 with final inspection of the house scheduled for August 17 and closing on August 18. We stayed in Arlington until the final inspection was satisfactorily completed and then took off for South Carolina. We drove both of the cars, with Mary leading the way, and arrived in Myrtle Beach about 11 p.m.. We were permanent, full-time Carolinians.

As soon as we got reasonably settled in our new home, we began to look into what the Grand Strand had to offer. Mary scoured the paper daily for what was happening. We soon found that there was much to do in the way of entertainment and interesting attractions. There were several community theater groups in the area, as well as professional theaters, and Broadway at the Beach was a large entertainment complex with many shops, restaurants, and other attractions. We explored most of these.

The first year we were in Myrtle Beach we joined about everything we heard of and bought season tickets to everything of the slightest interest. In the following months we realized that we had over extended ourselves—it's hard to be two places at the same time. We had so many tickets to plays, concerts, and other events, that we often had tickets to two events scheduled at the same time. In the following months we began to be more selective in what we subscribed to and bought.

For years I fought against computers—I thought they were just a passing fad and would go away. People at work kept wanting to put one on my desk; I refused. I attended computer classes, sometime more than one a year, but refused to accept the computer. Finally, in a weak moment I consented to have one of the monsters installed on my desk. At that time, I probably held the record, among government employees, for having attended the greatest number of computer classes without having a computer in my office. Little at a time I began to peck around on the thing. When I was finally convinced that it didn't carry any life-threatening disease, would not set me and the entire building on fire when I touched it, and that its gravest sin was replacing the Underwood typewriter, I began to take it seriously. By the time I retired I had fully accepted the computer and used it daily. I depended on it for writing letters (I became Mary's personal secretary), storing information, doing our taxes, and yes, e-mail and the Internet.

One day, while on the computer, I stumbled onto a web site through which you could locate people. I came across it strictly by accident—the first time I had ever been in a site of that nature. I thought: now that I'm in this place, who can I try to find? Immediately the name Arlton Hatch came into my mind. I had not thought of him in years and had not seen him in probably 50 years. I typed his name in the proper space, and instantly his complete address and telephone number popped up on the screen. I immediately dialed the number, and the lady who answered the telephone identified herself as Arlton's wife. He was not in at that time, but in a couple of hours he called me. What a remarkable experience! In our high school days we were closest of friends. Neither of us had a brother, but we became like brothers in those days.[15] We had a long conversation and vowed to keep in touch.

In early 2001 Mary and I visited Mary's sister who lived in Palm Desert, California. While there we drove to Escandido, where Arlton and his wife lived, for a visit. We had a delightful time and the two of us relived many experiences of our youth. It was a great reunion. The following year we were in California and once again visited Arlton. During the year between our visits Arlton had become very ill, and on this visit he was in a nursing home. It was a sad visit but we did enjoy some time together. About two weeks after our visit Arlton passed away.

In September 2001 Mary and I flew to England for a week, flying out of Charlotte, North Carolina, on US Airways

---

[15] See Chapter III, pages 51, 55, & 56-58.

Flight 94, for London. After a smooth and uneventful eight-hour flight, we landed at Gatwick Airport, about 8 a.m. Saturday morning. We rented a car, and were on our way. Gatwick Airport is located due south of London. Getting used to driving on the left side of the road on the busy thoroughfares around London gave us some anxious moments. However, we made our way around London to Route A1 and headed north. At Stamford we took Route A606 to Oakham and soon arrived at our destination, a very nice lake resort, about three hours north of London. Our accommodation for the week was a picturesque chalet overlooking Rutland Water (we would call it a lake). Each day we drove around the area enjoying the scenery and visiting points of interest: small villages, old churches, museums, castles, and manor houses. Although our chalet was well-appointed with kitchen facilities, except for breakfast, we ate most of our meals out. We especially enjoyed our lunches in the local pubs where the food was very good.

Tuesday, our third day in England, was filled with visiting new points of interest. Late in the afternoon, having had a full day of sightseeing, we returned to our chalet. As we opened the front door, we noticed an envelope on the floor just inside. Mary picked it up, opened it, and started to read—a very strange message.

> *The management wishes to express its sincere condolences, and will do all we can to help in any way to assist you in making any necessary arrangements. The local rector has said he would be available for counseling and the church will be open for prayer.*

What did this mean? A quick telephone call to the office elicited only a short statement: *Turn on your television.*

The British Broadcasting Corporation let us know in a very short time that the two World Trade Center buildings in New York City had been hit by airplanes hijacked by terrorists.

This was our introduction to the dastardly attacks of 9/11. Due to the difference in time in New York and England, the crashes had taken place only three or four hours before we learned of them, consequently, the early information was incomplete. In the next few days, BBC gave around-the-clock coverage to the tragedies. The coverage in England, those early days, was probably as complete as in the United States.

In the days following, we learned that 19 al-Qaeda terrorists had hijacked four commercial flights. American Airline Flight 11, to fly from Boston to Los Angeles, was crashed into the north tower of the World Trade Center at 8:46 a.m.[16] United Airline Flight 175, also scheduled to fly from Boston to Los Angeles, crashed into the south tower of the World Trade Center at 9:03 a.m.[17] Until the second tower was struck, it was assumed that the first crash was probably a tragic accident, but when the second tower was struck, it was evident that this was not the case. In a very short time word went out that American Airline Flight 77, scheduled from Washington Dulles Airport to Los Angeles, had crashed into the Pentagon in Arlington, Virginia, at 9:37 a.m.[18] As if these were not enough, the world soon heard that a fourth flight, United Airline Flight 93, had plowed into an empty field near Shanksville, Pennsylvania, shortly after 10 o'clock.[19] It was later learned that the destination of this flight was either the White House or the Capital building in Washington. In the following days the story of how the passengers of Flight 93 battled the terrorists was put together from the cell phone calls made by passengers to family members, friends, and colleagues. Their actions caused the plane to crash prematurely, thus saving the Washington target.

---

[16] The 9/11 Commission Report, W.W. Norton & Co., New York, p7.
[17] ibid, p8.
[18] ibid, p10.
[19] ibid, p14.

Initially, casualties at the World Trade Center were estimated as high as 6,000. The final count was just under 3,000, including the passengers and crews of the airplanes—81 passengers on American Flight 11, and 56 passengers on United Flight 175. American Flight 77 had a crew of six and 58 passengers when it crashed into the Pentagon. All were killed as well as many military and civilian personnel in the building. United Flight 93 had a crew of seven and 37 passengers as it crashed into the ground in Pennsylvania, killing all on board. The number of casualties from all of these incidents was between 3,000 and 4,000.

As Mary and I kept up with the news, we continued our sightseeing, although our attitude was somewhat somber. The people we met, recognizing us as Americans, would engage us in conversation about the terrorists' attacks and offer their sympathy. Everyone whom we met seemed very concerned about the incidents. As the week wore on, we began to think about our return trip home. Shortly after the attacks, all planes in the air over the U.S.A.` were ordered to land immediately, and for the next few days flights were cancelled and schedules drastically curtailed. Thursday I called US Airways to determine the status of our Saturday flight. I was told that its status was uncertain, and they would know more the next day.

Friday we checked out of our chalet and drove to London and checked into a hotel near the airport. That evening I called the airline. I was told that much of their fleet had been grounded in Canada, and the status of our flight would depend on how many aircraft they received Saturday morning. We passed a restless night and arrived at the airport early Saturday morning.

The inside of the terminal building was a madhouse—people hurrying in all directions, long lines of impatient people, airline representatives trying to maintain order, announcements over the speakers not heard over the din. We eventually made our way to the US Airways area. An airline representative told us that they had expected five planes but had received only two; this news dampened our hopes of departing that morning. We worked our way to the ticket counter and presented our tickets and passports. The ticket agent looked at our tickets and passports, while examining a document that she had in her hand, and said, "I'm sorry but you are not listed on this flight."

"This can't be," I responded, "look, there are our names, *Curtis Harlin* and *Mary Harlin*, and there is the correct flight number and today's date," pointing to our tickets. "Why are we not on this flight?"

"I'm sorry, but I cannot issue you boarding passes if your names are not on the passenger list," was the agent's reply. "You can take your tickets to the supervisor and talk to him, but if your names are not on the passenger list I'm working from, I can not issue boarding passes."

Mary took our tickets to see the supervisor while I stayed at the counter to watch our bags. The supervisor looked at our tickets and the passenger list and confirmed that our names were not on the list. Mary insisted that we had to be on that flight; there must be a mistake in the passenger list. Her persistence paid off: upon further examination of the passenger list the supervisor discovered that in printing the list, the computer had left off the first letter of our last names. On the list our names were *arlin*. When looking for our names on the list one would look for an "H" not an "A". The supervisor gave the ticket agent the OK and we were issued boarding passes. After much anxiety and frustration, we were on our way to board Flight 95 for Charlotte, North Carolina. How fortunate we were, only two US Airways flights out that day and we were on the first one.

We were lucky that our return flight was to Charlotte. Air traffic into the New York area, and other major cities on the east coast, was still not well established. The man in the seat next to me was scheduled to go to New Jersey, but his flight was cancelled so he took our flight just to get back to the

United States. He had no idea how he would get from Charlotte to New Jersey.

We had a relaxing flight into Charlotte, arriving about four o'clock in the afternoon. We found our car and drove the three hours to our home in Myrtle Beach. Our home had never been so beautiful and hospitable. Reflecting on the past few days, we felt that we had probably had our last trip abroad, at least to England—getting too old for driving on the wrong side of the road, understanding their signs, and maneuvering the round-abouts. We do enjoy their country, *but there is no place on this earth as good as the US of A!*

XV

Retrospection

In the summer of 2002 I signed up for an art class in oil painting. Many years before I had tried my hand at painting and enjoyed it, but I had not done anything since then. Through the years, I had wanted to take it up again but never found the right time to do it. When I read about the local adult classes in the paper, I knew I had to try it. The instructor, Jim Dyson, was a great guy, a wonderful artist, and an excellent teacher. I bought all of the necessary equipment and became very serious about my artistic endeavor. With Jim's help and encouragement, within the next couple of years I produced several nice paintings. I joined a local art guild and entered my work in several of their shows. I won a red ribbon (second place) in the novice class at one of the shows. My greatest accomplishment was a painting that Mary's sister, Reita, "commissioned" me to do. It was of seven of her grandchildren on a beach. The painting was a 30" by 24" oil on canvas. Before I presented the original to Reita, I had a 24" by 20" reproduction made for myself. I have had many compliments on the painting.

Our years in Myrtle Beach have been very enjoyable. Mary loves the beach and tries to walk a couple of miles almost every day, weather permitting. She prefers to walk during low tide. In order to keep up with the tides she has a tide clock that tells the hours that have passed since the high and low tides and the number of hours until the next tide. When we were preparing to move to Myrtle Beach, Mary looked forward to walking the beach with Heidi. Soon after arriving in Myrtle Beach, she and Heidi and I went to the beach to introduce Heidi to the pleasure of walking on the sandy beach. We soon discovered that this environment was not to Heidi's liking. She set her four feet in the sand and would not move. We don't know if it was the sound of the waves or what caused her problem, but it was apparent that she would have nothing to do with the beach. We repeated the experiment a couple of times with the same negative results. After that Mary never took her to the beach.

We have continued cruising. During our six years in Myrtle Beach we have taken cruises from Santiago, Chili, around the cape to Buenos Aries; from Los Angeles to Acapulco, Mexico; a transatlantic cruise from Fort Lauderdale, Florida, to Barcelona, Spain; and a Pacific islands cruise. We have also taken several land trips to various places in the United States. We are beginning to slow down on the traveling, though. As we age we have less interest in leaving home, and it is getting more difficult to find places we would be interested in that we have not already visited.

A year or two after we moved to Myrtle Beach I discovered the Life Long Learning Society at Coastal Carolina University, a local state university. The society offers a wide variety of non-credit courses for seniors. I have taken one or two of these courses every year, usually computer or writing courses. In 2003 I was elected to the Advisory Board of the society, became secretary of the board, and served for two years. During that time I made a number of friends and learned to appreciate the role of CCU in the community.

The year after we moved to our new home, the builder turned the Property Owners' Association over to the owners. During the development of the property, the developer ran the show. After all homes were built, and had owners, his role was completed. I was elected to the Board of Directors of the association, initially served as Secretary of the board, followed by President the last year I was on the board.

In 2004 I was elected to the board of the Community Concerts Association. This position was short-lived as the association disbanded shortly after my election. At one time though, I was on three boards, which kept me very busy. Currently I have no community responsibilities and that is the way I want to keep it. Mary and I are active in our church; Mary is a lector and ecumenical minister; I usher and count money.

In 2005, Mary's family gave me a surprise 85th birthday party. What a party! It lasted two days. Day one Mary and I drove to David and Sandy's home in Florence, and I was surprised by being greeted by a host of family. They came from California, Pennsylvania, Michigan, and Indiana. We had a great feast with David doing his usual excellent job on the grill. It was a great day.

The following day we all gathered at our home for drinks and munchies and then went to a nice restaurant in Conway between Florence and Myrtle Beach. We had a private room and what a surprise when I entered. All around the room, posted on the walls, were posters of events and activities of my life. David and Sandy had had the posters made from information Mary had given them—an unfinished copy of this autobiography, my high school yearbook, and numerous newspaper clipping I had saved during the years. I was literally speechless. The dinner was excellent. I will never forget my 85th, which was the most fantastic birthday I have ever had.

Shortly after my 85th birthday I had an appointment with my dentist for a regular checkup and cleaning. I said to him, "Dr. Bob, I'm going to live to be 100 years old so you have to guarantee these teeth for another fifteen years."

He responded, "How often do you come for cleaning?"

"Every six months."

"Well, you better change that to every four months."

The period in which I have lived has been one of the most fantastic eras of all time. Things have been accomplished that in earlier years were only dreamed of. Many things that were only subjects of science-fiction writers in 1920, the year of my birth, are common today. In the areas of communication, transportation, and medicine the advances, during my lifetime, have been unequaled in any other period of history.

In my early years, communication by telephone was by use of an instrument through which you called an operator who would connect you to the party you wished to call. The common telephone, such as in our home, was an upright instrument that sat on a desk or table and you spoke into it, with a separate receiver attached by a cord that you put to your ear to listen through. In some areas, especially in rural areas, the telephones were large wall-mounted boxes, and the caller contacted the operator by turning a crank that was on the side of the box. Places that had telephone service had transmission wires on poles strung in the roads or alleys throughout the area. The quality of the service depended a lot on your location, and frequently storms or other occurrences would disrupt the service.

The contrast today in telephone service is remarkable. Telephones are in practically every home in the country, regardless of location, and most homes have more than one conveniently located in the house. No longer are callers confined to a stationary instrument connected to wires and cables; the modern-day cell phone is easily carried in your purse or pocket and can be used almost any place. Almost every place you go—on streets, in public buildings, in cars— you see people talking on their cell phones. The youngest and the oldest seem to be addicted to them.

Radio and television have come of age during my lifetime. In my earliest years, radio was a novelty not found in many homes.[20] Today practically every home has several radios— in the living room, the den, the bedrooms, the kitchen—and they are not confined to the home or workplace. Practically

---

[20] See Chapter II, pp. 24-25.

every current model automobile has a radio; portable radios are commonly carried outside, especially by teenagers. Today even the smallest community has a radio station. The numerous radio networks broadcast events and entertainment programs to all parts of the world

Television was not common until the late 1940s and early 1950s. Today even the humblest home has a television set. Television dominates news transmission, broadcasting events as they happen around the world. Entertainment programs of all kinds are featured around the clock on the television networks. Television watching dominates many homes every evening, some say to the determent of reading and other learning skills, especially among the young people. Nevertheless, television is the dominant factor today in home entertainment and news transmission.

And, yes, there are computers.

References to man using crude devices to perform calculations are found in early history. In modern times the development of analog computers in the 1930s and 1940s was thought to be the ultimate in this field of technology. These computers were large, requiring a lot of space, and were not very flexible in the types of problems they could handle. The invention of the integrated circuit and the microprocessor led to small low-cost computers that were practical for the average person. By 1980 personal computers were common and their use and utility has continued to grow. Many manufacturing, transportation, and other commercial operations depend on computers. But the most astounding aspect of the computer story is their wide use by individuals. Desktop and laptop computers are everywhere. With the advent of e-mail and the internet, personal computers are no longer devices for doing calculations, although they have this capability; they have become communication instruments. Maybe something will come along in the future to overshadow computers, but now, as I write this on my computer, they seem to be the ultimate communication machine.

In the first few years of my life, long-distance travel was not easy. The automobile was rather common, but traveling long distances by automobile was sometimes difficult; roads were not good and mechanical problems were common.[21] Those who traveled abroad had no choice but the steam ship, which took days to cross the ocean. Aviation was in its infancy with very limited scheduled passenger service. The choice for traveling long distances on land was the passenger train that took considerable time.

How different today: we truly are a mobile society. The automobile is everywhere, city streets are crowded with them, and on the highways one can travel hundreds of miles a day at speeds of 70 miles an hour and greater. The automobile is highly reliable with few mechanical problems. The option for long distance land travel, besides the automobile, is by airplane. Regional, national, and world wide commercial carriers whisk passengers across the skies at speeds exceeding 500 miles per hour comfortably and safely. Travel across the oceans is within reach of much of our population on luxurious cruise ships that provide excellent entertainment and comfort.

We are now in the space age, traveling to places in the universe that were seen only through a telescope a few years ago. It all began on October 4, 1957, when the Soviet Union launched Sputnik 1, the first artificial satellite to orbit the Earth. This event ushered in the space race between the United States and the Soviets. The United States surpassed the Soviets with the Apollo program landing Neil Armstrong the first man on the moon. Since then many launches by the USA have reached new heights and explored other planets in our solar system. A permanent space station has been built and is occupied by personnel from the cooperating countries,

---

[21] See Chapter II, pp. 28-30.

including the U.S.A. Invaluable data is collected from the space station. In the next few years it is expected that commercial passenger flights in space will be available to those who have the desire—and money.

Life expectancy for a white male born in 1920 was 56 years; in 2003 it was 75 years. This increase in our life expectancy is due, largely, to the great advances in modern day medicine. Of course, better diets and living conditions have also contributed, but without the modern medical miracles our long lives would not be possible.

Those childhood diseases—whooping cough, measles, chickenpox—that all children were expected to have, when I was growing up, are almost unheard of now, thanks to modern vaccines. Polioyelitis, the dreaded disease that crippled so many young people in the past, has been completely wiped out of our society. The advances in surgery are beyond belief. Heart and kidney transplants, as well as repair and replacement of other human organs, are performed almost routinely by skilled surgeons today. When an older person's knees and hips wear out they can now be replaced. These and other many advances in modern medicine make our lives happier, more useful, and longer.

We all have had the experience of going to a doctor the first time and having to fill out the lengthy forms detailing our medical history. A year or so ago I was referred to an arthritis specialist. After filling out the form I returned it to the nurse. Scanning it she said:

"You don't take any medication?"

"No," I responded.

"You don't take anything for high blood pressure or cholesterol or anything?"

"No," I repeated.

Her look, as she turned away, was one of disbelief.

One of my greatest blessings has been my good health. I do have the usual aches and pains that come with ageing, but I have none of the life threatening ailments that are so common among people of my age. I thank God every day for his many blessings, especially for the blessing of good health

With all the great things that have happened in the world during my lifetime, there is no doubt that I have lived in the most fantastic era of all time. Having completed my first 85 years, I now look forward to the next 85 years.